The Art of Mindful UX

UX Design Through the Buddha's Eyes

Eric Infanti

eric@yoga-wod.com

The Art of Mindful UX: UX Design Through the Buddha's Eyes/ Eric Infanti. —1st ed.

ISBN: 9798874124519

Contents

Conclusion:

Dedication

In gratitude. In the hallowed echoes of silent wisdom, a dedication unfurls like petals to the meditation teachers who have gifted the treasury of their enlightenment. Their path, a luminescent tapestry, paves the way for us to tread, igniting the lanterns along our own sacred journey, marking a trail for those who will dance in our footsteps.

To those souls who entrusted me with the alchemy of guidance, teaching, and love, we traverse a mystical sojourn together. Our steps echo a magical cadence, orchestrating a symphony of healing light that we, as custodians, cast upon the world. In this dance, we learn, and perhaps more crucially, unlearn — shedding layers to stand more authentically in the radiance of our true selves.

I Experience these words entwined with realms beyond my own, deeply anchored within, a manifestation that rises and seeks sanctuary within my Soul. A force that metamorphoses me, demanding authenticity in the face of any alchemical transformation.

This "force," a rendezvous with the Divine, I am fortunate to cradle in the vessel of love through the mediums that carry them. Despite its fearsome nature, it is equally blissful and tranquil, coursing through me to radiate love and illuminate others.

The narratives of an untamed, lively heart, a Soul laid bare in vulnerability, offered to others for their embrace.

As this messenger, I embark on a creative odyssey to impact both myself and others on their unique journeys to the highest echelons of life. To act upon the innate human drive to create, to design, to delve into the profound recesses of their own Souls.

This is a tribute... a tribute to the gifts bestowed upon us, a commitment to nurture these gifts with grace and elegance within the unfolding process of learning to trust.

And so, it unfolds... Eric Infanti

Foundations of Synergy

EXPLORING THE NEXUS

There is a nexus, a meeting place that is both profound and transformative, in the brilliant voyage of design, where purpose meets creation. Here, we find the meeting point of the timeless doctrines of the Buddha with the modern field of *User Experience (UX) Design.*

At this crossroads of apparently unrelated realms, we set sail on an exploratory adventure that will lead us to greater insight into the human condition and, by extension, design.

Imagine, if you will, a blank canvas where the artist's conscious movements lead each brushstroke to a harmonious final product that speaks to the user's spirit. *Mindful user experience design* is an art form that goes beyond the usual confines of design to tap into fundamental human qualities like empathy, ethics, and purpose. It is a delicate balancing act, where the measured practicality of UX design meets the calm contemplation of Buddha's teachings.

This book delves into the origins of this harmony by investigating how the Eightfold Path, central to the teachings of the Buddha, can shed light on the concepts of user experience design. Following the teachings of the Buddha about the significance of having the right perspective, intention, speech, action, livelihood, effort, mindfulness, and concentration, we will learn how these principles can give our design process meaning beyond just making things work.

This section's chapters are like stepping-stones on a journey leading to revelation. At the intersection of UX design concepts and the teachings of the Buddha, we begin to uncover the ideologies that not only coexist but also enrich each other.

Along the way, we will encounter deep discoveries and debates as we investigate the points of agreement and disagreement between different ideologies.

Picture yourself as you peruse these pages strolling through a garden of thoughts, *where every idea is a flower just waiting to blossom under your kind care*. Here we will explore the concepts of user experience design, but more than that, we will strive to create experiences that resonate with users on an emotional and intellectual level.

Let us go out on this adventure together, prepared to investigate the intersection of user experience design and the teachings of the Buddha. Join me in practicing mindful UX, where each decision we make as designers contributes to a society that is more empathetic, inclusive, and peaceful.

CHAPTER 1

Inception of Harmonious Design

1.1 Confluence of Philosophies: UX and Buddha's Path

We find ourselves at a rare crossroads — the harmonious intersection of User Experience (UX) Design and the profound, age-old teachings of Buddha — in the enormous and ever-expanding universe of digital creation, where every element of design has the potential to unite souls and minds.

This amazing marriage creates a link between two seemingly different worlds. The contemporary digital landscape is, on the one hand, a world of perpetual invention and technical advancement that pulses with the pace of development and change.

On the other hand, there is the calm and ageless realm of Buddhist wisdom, *which has its roots in the quest for enlightenment and a deep comprehension of human nature.* The methodical, analytical techniques of UX design blend with the profound spirituality of Buddhism in this hallowed space, creating a synergy that goes beyond the conventional bounds of design and unlocks new possibilities for user engagement and experience.

We set off on a journey that is both an inquiry and a revelation as we investigate this relationship. The user-centered design methodologies and their painstaking approaches start to dance to a different melody — one that resonates with the spiritual melodies of Buddhist teachings.

These approaches place an emphasis on:
- usability,
- accessibility,
- and engagement.

This dance adds a new level of significance and purpose to the digital experience; it is more than just a surface-level alignment of concepts. It is a profound, soulful union.

The Buddha's teachings provide a rich conceptual context for reimagining UX design approaches, with an emphasis on mindfulness, compassion, and the realization of the interconnectedness of all beings.

> This reimagining results in a digital product that is both cerebrally stimulating and emotionally impactful, capable of being both efficient and effective while also possessing a feeling of empathy and spiritual depth.

A new paradigm in the field of digital design is born out of this perfect marriage. It is a paradigm where vivid pixels and clean lines of code in digital interfaces become more than just tools for functionality; they become channels for deep understanding and human connection.

This domain reimagines every facet of the user experience, from the design of a webpage to the functionality of an application, using the prism of spirituality. This viewpoint challenges us as designers and makers to think more deeply about the emotional and spiritual resonance of our work in addition to the pragmatic considerations of usability and aesthetics.

We have a responsibility to design not only for the physical senses but also for the human spirit. We want to make digital experiences that are journeys of learning, connection, and discovery rather than just informational or amusing exchanges.

We discover a way to create digital experiences that are genuinely holistic — experiences that satisfy the mind, the senses, and the spirit — in this blending of UX and the teachings of the Buddha.

The Philosophical Tapestry:
Unraveling the Eightfold Path in UX

We are creating a distinctive philosophical tapestry in the rich and complex terrain where the fundamental ideas of User Experience (UX) Design meet with the profound teachings of Buddha. This colorful, multi-layered tapestry weaves the Eightfold Path of Buddhism and the noble truths together to create a framework that is both practical and illuminating.

- The right view,
- right intention,
- right speech,
- right action,
- right livelihood,
- right effort,
- right mindfulness,
- and right concentration

are all components of this path that have a strong resonance with the core ideas of UX design. Together, they create a harmonious blend that enhances our method of developing digital experiences.

The 'correct view' concept, which is central to Buddhist philosophy and promotes a precise knowledge of the nature of reality and human perceptions, is at the center of this tapestry. This is in line with the fundamental UX design principle of having a thorough understanding of user viewpoints and experiences. This alignment involves more than just understanding the user's wants and requirements; it also entails developing a comprehensive understanding of the user's reality, including their emotions, behaviors, struggles, and victories.

Adopting this 'correct vision' enables designers to produce solutions that deeply resonate with the user's real context and circumstance, in addition to being functionally useful. This methodology goes beyond the surface level of user preferences, delving deep into the core of the user experience to uncover significant and transforming insights.

Comparably, the concept of "right intention" in Buddhism, which supports deeds motivated by kindness, compassion, and moral principles, has an equivalent in the field of UX design. According to this notion, designers should incorporate intents into their work that go beyond just aesthetic appeal or technical skill.

Making sure that each design choice supports the principles of moral accountability, social good, and positive effect is all part of creating with a conscience. This connection with 'proper intention' pushes us to think about the bigger picture and ask questions about how our designs impact society and the environment in addition to the user.

This inspires us to create with compassion, imbuing our works with a sense of moral purpose that improves, upholds, and enhances the lives of others who come into contact with them.

> As we work through this conceptual maze, we see how every stage of the Eightfold Path provides a different perspective that allows us to improve our UX practices.

Every step on this route points us in the direction of a more conscientious, moral, and comprehensive approach to design, from "right speech," which promotes compassionate and transparent communication, to "right action," which supports designs that are constructive and non-harmful. In the context of UX, this journey along the Eightfold Path is about more than just improving the user experience. *It is about taking it to the next level, where spirituality and technology meet to create digital experiences that are deeply human, wise, and compassionate in addition to being effective and engaging.*

Ethical Design: The Intersection of Right Intention and User-Centricity

A deeper exploration of the relationship between UX design and Buddha's teachings leads us to a pivotal point at which the fundamental principles of UX design, user-centricity, and "right intention," which form the basis of Buddhist ethics, converge.

This intersection is more than just a meeting of pathways; rather, it represents the union of a strong sense of moral obligation and altruism with the specific goal of producing compelling and user-friendly digital experiences. *Here, the UX ethos of prioritizing the needs and experiences of the user in the design process aligns with the*

Buddhist principle of "right intention," which exhorts people to act with kindness, compassion, and a strong sense of ethical duty. This alignment challenges us to dig underneath the surface of utility and beauty to the underlying values and impacts of our products, which leads to a deeper reflection and introspection of our design aims.

This area transforms the way we approach design. It turns into a process imbued with a sense of moral purpose, in which every choice, component, and interaction is evaluated for both its practicality and its ethical consequences. This ethical approach to UX design is about designing with a conscience, which goes beyond simply making interfaces that are simple and enjoyable to use.

We must think about how our designs may uphold integrity and purpose while also encouraging kindness, respect, and honesty. It is a pledge to take into account the wider effects of our designs on users' well-being as well as the well-being of the community at large, in addition to attending to their immediate requirements. This entails considering how our designs may uphold diversity, safeguard privacy, promote positive behavior, and advance societal progress as a whole.

Furthermore, the idea that our designs should be both vehicles for good change and instruments for task accomplishment arises from the junction of "right intention" and user-centricity. This gives every user a chance to positively impact and inspire others. Our designs may become a force for good, reflecting our dedication to fostering a more compassionate and responsible digital world, whether it is through thoughtful content, materials supplied responsibly, or environmentally friendly processes.

This ethical aspect of UX design forces us to reassess and hone our goals on a regular basis to make sure that our work promotes more harmony and balance in both society and the lives of users. It is a journey to make digital experiences that uplift, inspire, and nourish the human spirit in addition to connecting and engaging people.

Mindfulness and UX: Crafting Conscious Experiences

We come across the transforming power of mindfulness in the paths that intersect between UX design and the profound teachings of Buddha. *With this integration, the design paradigm will change significantly from making interfaces to creating experiences that profoundly connect with the mental and emotional environment of the user.*

Design mindfulness is a philosophy that involves approaching the creative process with a profound understanding of how it will affect the user's mental processing rather than just a technique. It is about addressing the most nuanced facets of the human experience by going beyond the boundaries of design and utility. Every design element in this case has been thoroughly evaluated for how it might impact the user's emotional and mental states in addition to its aesthetic appeal and usability.

With every color, shape, and interaction carefully chosen to contribute to an intuitive and spiritually uplifting overall experience, this mindful approach to UX design turns the process into a more deliberate and conscious act.

Deeper exploration of this mindful method reveals that designing with awareness extends beyond the component parts of an interface. It includes every step of the user's journey, from the initial point of contact to the continuing exchange.

It all comes down to designing a peaceful, easy-to-use digital environment that seamlessly integrates ease and tranquility into the whole experience. Every change in this area is seamless, every communication is comforting and clear, and every action moves users closer to developing a stronger bond with the digital world. This thoughtful incorporation into UX design results in interfaces that are not only easy to use but also uplifted and emotionally supportive, offering a haven in the digital world where people can interact in a way that is more meaningful and satisfying.

We are at the start of a new age in digital creativity as we wrap up our investigation into the fusion of mindfulness and UX design. This is a time when the most recent technical developments coexist peacefully with the ageless practice of mindfulness. This chapter has taken us on a voyage into a world in which design is not only a career but also a route to enlightenment, and where developing digital experiences turns into a morally and compassionate practice.

Let us take the knowledge and ideas from this special convergence with us as we continue on our path as designers in the digital age. Let us endeavor to design experiences that speak to the depths of the human spirit as well as the screen, using not just our technological expertise and artistic vision but also our hearts and minds.

Through this journey, we embrace the potential of mindfulness to revolutionize design, producing digital experiences that are not just interactive and captivating but also nourishing, peaceful, and uplifting — a veritable expression of the harmony that exists between spiritual understanding and technology.

1.2 Profound Insights and Contentions

We set out on an extensive and winding road to merge the revered teachings of Buddha with the principles of user experience design. This journey transports us to a world where cutting-edge technological design meets age-old spiritual knowledge, forging a terrain brimming with deep understanding and provocative debates.

We are not on a straight and predictable road; rather, it is a meandering one with spurts of profound insight and difficult, reflective periods interwoven. The more we explore this unfamiliar intersection, the more we realize how difficult it is to find common ground between the more meditative and contemplative aspects of Buddhist philosophy and the more rapid-fire realm of user-centric design.

We might think of this adventure as a quest through a digital forest. As we make our way through this forest, the intermittent bursts of understanding's dappled sunlight illuminate our path with clarity and vision. But equally striking are the specters of paradox and disagreement, which beg us to stop, think, and tackle more profound and intricate issues.

Rather than being a theoretical or academic exercise, this investigation pushes us to put the peaceful teachings of Buddha into practice in the real world of digital design. Every step of the way, we are meeting new intersections and misunderstandings along the path; there are times when Buddhist philosophy and UX design concepts are completely congruent, and other times when they could not be more different.

These areas of disagreement are not roadblocks but rather possibilities for more in-depth investigation and comprehension. They make us think critically about our design beliefs and processes, which in turn encourages us to break out of our comfort zones and consider alternative perspectives. We must think about how the Buddhist ideals of detachment and mindfulness may coexist with the internet industry's incessant quest for user happiness as we make our way across this complex terrain.

> How can the eternal truths preached by Buddha coexist with the incessant innovation and change that is inherent in technology? As we set out on our adventure, these are the questions that will serve as our compass, pushing us to reconcile two seemingly irreconcilable realities.

The road of integrating UX design with Buddhist principles is not one of discovering an ideal synthesis or eradicating all inconsistencies, as we come to understand on this journey. Rather, it is about welcoming the variety of viewpoints that this convergence brings. What this means is that we may create digital experiences in a more holistic, compassionate, and ethical way by combining modern design approaches with ancient wisdom.

Embracing the interplay between design, philosophy, practice, and thought, this journey pushes us to be versatile thinkers and designers. Our journey has been filled with both moments of clarity and moments of darkness, but with each step we have taken, we have become wiser and more sophisticated in our approach to design and life in general.

The Intersection of Innovation and Timelessness

We find an interesting meeting point between the ever-evolving field of technical innovation and the eternal domain of Buddhist precepts. This juncture offers a singular chance for synthesis while also presenting a startling contrast. UX design is one area that is closely related to the swift advances in technology and is always changing to meet the demands of users and keep up with the latest developments in digital technology.

It is a world that thrives on *the new, the better, and the next, where innovation is not just valued but also necessary.* The ancient wisdom of the Buddha's teachings, on the other hand, is a body of knowledge and practice that has withstood the test of millennia and is unwavering in its fundamental ideas and ideals. Here, the emphasis is on ageless principles and practices that continue to be relevant and true throughout time, providing a solid basis for moral and spiritual direction.

Despite its obvious absurdity, this intersection provides significant insight into the possibility of peaceful cohabitation and mutual enrichment. The problem of combining these two worlds — of bringing the quick-paced, constantly-evolving world of UX design into line with the timeless, unchanging substance of spiritual wisdom—gives rise to conflict or creative tension.

How can we create technologically advanced experiences that have the profundity and clarity of age-old wisdom? Finding a medium ground that respects and makes use of the advantages present in both areas is crucial. It entails developing digital experiences that are not only cutting edge and innovative in terms of technology but also profoundly representative of timeless human values. These experiences should be as thoughtful and inventive as they are empathetic and forward-thinking.

We have a dual responsibility in this endeavor: guardians in preserving and integrating the eternal wisdom of Buddhist teachings, and pioneers in pushing the frontiers of what is possible in digital design. This dual function necessitates a kind of ballet, a delicate balancing act, where each innovative move must be accompanied by a foundation in moral and spiritual values.

It is about creating digital experiences that are not just more functionally advanced but also more spiritually enlightening by bridging the gaps between the ancient and the new, the fleeting and the eternal. This junction forces us to reconsider how we approach design and pushes us to imagine a time where spirituality and technology coexist peacefully and flourish side by side, resulting in a digital environment that is as uplifting to the human spirit as it is to the human experience.

Embracing Ethical Challenges in UX

We enter a world full of ethical issues and difficulties when we combine the deep teachings of Buddha with the delicate dance of UX design. This leg of the trip delves deeply into the moral fiber of UX design, where each choice and innovation has significant ethical ramifications. In this dynamic world of digital design, we often find ourselves in morally challenging situations as designers.

These might range from complex concerns about data security and privacy to the psychological effects of our designs on consumers. These problems are more than just technical difficulties; they are ethical conundrums that force us to stop and consider the wider ramifications of our work. *Buddha's teachings, which are based on morality, compassion, and good deeds, provide direction in these uncertain times. They give us a moral compass that makes navigating the tricky ethical landscape of the digital business easier.*

The route is not without controversy, though. When the ethical principles embedded in Buddhist philosophy come into contact with the business goals and pragmatic realities of the tech industry, a major dilemma arises.

In a sector that prioritizes innovation, user experience, and financial gain, how can we continue to uphold a strong commitment to moral values? How can we create user-engaging experiences without crossing the line into deception or exploitation?

These are the important issues that come up when we try to match our work with moral principles. It can be challenging to strike a careful balance between ethical integrity and financial success. *It necessitates in-depth reflection and a readiness to question the existing quo, asking not only how but also why we create.*

We are encouraged to be ethical stewards of the digital sphere in addition to being designers as we tackle these moral dilemmas. This position necessitates making a deliberate effort to incorporate moral issues into each design phase. It entails moving past merely following rules and laws to a place of true ethical commitment, where users' welfare is prioritized above all else. It entails producing designs that are not just captivating and user-friendly but also considerate of privacy, open and honest in their intentions, and supportive of users' general well-being.

By accepting these moral dilemmas, we pave the way for a more comprehensive approach to UX design, one that strikes a balance between moral obligation and technical innovation as well as between ethical mindfulness and user engagement. This method not only makes our ideas seem more credible and trustworthy, but it also unites our work as professionals with a deeper, more significant goal: creating digital experiences that are not just efficient and entertaining, but also morally and respectfully sound.

The Paradox of User-Centricity and Detachment

The idea of user-centricity is a compass in the dynamic and always-changing field of UX design. This design approach aims to make every component of the digital experience as engaging, simple to use, and fulfilling as possible by prioritizing the requirements, preferences, and experiences of the user early in the process.

The constant emphasis on the user is what propels innovation and quality in the UX industry. But an interesting paradox appears when we examine this idea from the calm and introspective prism of Buddhist teachings. Buddhism places a strong emphasis on the idea of detachment and the realization that all experiences in this world are temporary. This viewpoint poses a special challenge: *how can we balance the Buddhist ideal of non-attachment and awareness of life's transience with the objective of developing incredibly engaging and fulfilling user experiences?*

This paradox challenges us to investigate the meaning of responsible and mindful design in further detail. It pushes us to design user experiences that are both captivating and delightful, while simultaneously bringing the deeper realities of human existence to light. Our goal in this field is to create rich, immersive digital experiences that avoid encouraging excessive attachment or diverting attention from life's more important components. It involves designing a user experience that balances empathy for the user and responsiveness to their requirements with an awareness of the transience and fluidity of the digital world. This method pushes us to think about how our designs will affect users' entire lives and well-being in the long run, not just the immediate one.

We find ourselves at the nexus of two worlds as we explore this paradox: the meditative, introspective world of Buddhist philosophy and the dynamic, user-focused field of UX design. This crossroads is a hub for development and creativity rather than a source of strife. We have the chance to learn more about what it means to design with awareness and purpose. We may infuse our work with a fresh perspective on mindfulness and ethical thinking by adopting the teachings of Buddhism. It is up to us to think about how our designs contribute to the broader good, encouraging awareness, balance, and ethical responsibility, in addition to how they immediately satisfy the demands of users. It is not the goal of this investigation to resolve every conflict or provide conclusive answers.

Instead, it is an ongoing process of discovering, modifying, and improving our method of design. It is an expedition that enhances our work, broadens our perspective on the human condition, and helps to build a digital environment that is not just interesting and useful but also kind, thoughtful, and morally upright. We embrace the contradictions in this never-ending journey and work to strike a healthy balance by fusing the best aspects of both worlds to produce digital experiences that are genuinely significant and enriching for life.

CHAPTER 2

The Essence of the Design Journey

2.1 Bridging Wisdoms: UX and Buddhist Philosophy

We come across a unique and alluring combination in the intriguing and enlightening voyage that combines the fundamental ideas of Buddhist philosophy with the principles of UX design. This merging unites two seemingly disparate trajectories: the pragmatic, outcome-oriented field of UX design and the reflective, introspective realm of Buddhism.

This combination creates a singular link between the abstract, philosophical insights of ancient spirituality and the practical, empirical techniques of contemporary design. It is a synthesis that challenges us to think more broadly about design and push the bounds of conventional UX methodologies into unexplored ground.

Here, in this beautiful convergence, the timeless wisdom contained in Buddhist teachings blends harmoniously with the methodical, user-centric methodologies of UX design. The end-product is a complex, nuanced fusion that elevates both fields and shows how the ideas driving meaningful, mindful living and good design are not mutually exclusive but rather interwoven strands of a bigger, more complex fabric.

This union is a practical strategy that gives the technical parts of UX design a deeper feeling of purpose and reflection, going beyond a mere theoretical overlap. The incorporation of Buddhist philosophy adds a deeper level of understanding to the field of user experience (UX), where user contentment, efficiency, and functionality are crucial factors.

It demands a design approach that prioritizes developing a quality of mindfulness, compassion, and ethical thinking in addition to problem-solving and smooth user experiences. This method pushes designers to consider the wider effects of their work on the user's overall experience and well-being, pushing them to see beyond the immediate usefulness and visual appeal of their works. It involves creating digital experiences that, in addition to being utilitarian, also speak to users' emotions and spiritual needs; they should not just help people complete tasks but also improve their lives.

Essentially, this fusion of Buddhist philosophy with UX design signifies a revolutionary path for both disciplines. It challenges UX professionals to take a more comprehensive approach to their work, taking into account not only the technical specifications of their projects but also the human elements — the feelings, ideas, and more fundamental needs of the users.

In addition, it demonstrates the timeless wisdom of Buddhism's teachings' relevance and flexibility in tackling modern issues by enabling them to find fresh interpretations and uses in the digital age. This convergence demonstrates the potential of fusing spiritual ideas with practical knowledge to provide a design approach that is thorough, compassionate, and profoundly rooted in the human experience.

We advance our understanding of the human condition and develop our skills as designers as we travel this integrated route, making a positive impact on a world where technology and spirituality come together to produce more meaningful, thoughtful, and rewarding experiences.

The Wisdom of Mindfulness in Design

The key idea of mindfulness is crucial to the integration of UX design with the deep teachings of Buddhism. This idea, which is central to Buddhist philosophy, gives the UX design process a profoundly transformational quality. Beyond the traditional emphasis on utility and aesthetics, mindfulness in design encourages designers to participate in a more thoughtful, reflective creative process. This method encourages designers to think about how each component of their work affects the user's emotional and cognitive well-being, which demands for a heightened awareness of the present moment.

It is a request to look past the obvious and gain a deeper understanding of and empathy for the user's experience. This translates into creating digital experiences that are not just functional or aesthetically beautiful but also peaceful, enriching, and accurately represent the requirements and emotional condition of the user. In the often-hectic digital universe, such attentive design provides a haven of peace and contemplation for the user, fostering them.

It takes a mental change to integrate mindfulness into UX design; one must stop considering design as a problem-solving exercise and begin to perceive it as an act of empathy and compassion. When designers include mindfulness into their work, they set out to create experiences that are deeply aware of the subtleties of the human experience rather than just being user-centric in the conventional sense.

This method encourages a deeper and more meaningful relationship between the user and the digital environment. The intricacies of mental states, the nuances of human emotions, and the unsaid demands that lay under the surface are all considered in mindful design.

It is about realizing that every computer interface interaction can affect a user's mood, stress level, and general sense of well-being in a subtle but meaningful way. By placing a high priority on mindfulness, designers may produce situations that not only address real-world issues but also foster emotional harmony, mental clarity, and tranquility.

The application of mindfulness to design is wise not only for improving user experience but also for reframing design's place in the digital age.

- It transforms the design process from a technical undertaking into a comprehensive, people-focused activity.
- Digital worlds produced using this mindfulness-driven method are intuitive, captivating, nurturing, and rewarding.
- It creates environments that connect with the user on a deeper level, environments that are not just easy to navigate and operate but also sympathetic and calming.
- By bridging the gap between technology and human experience, mindfulness integration into UX design promotes digital solutions that are not just efficient but also emotionally and spiritually enlightening.

In addition to being technologically sophisticated, designers who adopt this mindful approach help create a digital environment that is caring, considerate and tuned into the deeper rhythms of human existence.

Harmonizing UX with Buddhist Ethics

One important component that shows up in the complex interaction between Buddhist philosophy and UX design is the incorporation of ethical concepts. *Buddhism provides a strong moral compass that can direct the UX design process because it is firmly based in the principles of moral behavior, compassion, and the pursuit of wisdom.*

This integration gives UX design a stronger feeling of moral and social duty than just putting concepts side by side. It blends them harmoniously. We establish a paradigm where digital experiences are not only functional and efficient but also based in morality and social consciousness by incorporating Buddhist ethical concepts into UX design.

This method goes beyond the conventional goals of user satisfaction and business success, which forces us to think about the wider effects of our work on the welfare of users and society as a whole.

Designing with intention has a new meaning in this harmonious environment. It entails making a deliberate effort to make sure that digital products are agents of positive change as well as convenient or engaging tools. This entails designing experiences that are inclusive of all users while taking into account their varied requirements and backgrounds.

Eric Infanti

> It entails creating user interfaces that respect the autonomy, privacy, and dignity of users in addition to being aesthetically pleasing. To put it simply, developing digital environments that are inclusive, sympathetic, and appreciative of the human condition is the essence of harmonizing UX with Buddhist ideals. It involves fostering a digital environment that upholds moral and humanitarian principles that improve human existence in addition to design utility and aesthetics.

It is both illuminating and difficult to include Buddhist ethics into UX design.

- It necessitates constant learning, adaptation, and development on the part of both professionals and everyday people looking to positively influence the world through their work.
- By incorporating Buddhist concepts into our design processes, we can produce digital experiences that not only meet users' technical and aesthetic needs but also uplift and nourish their minds and spirits.
- Through this method, we are creating experiences that speak to the deepest desires of human existence rather than just creating interfaces.
- Our work helps create a digital environment that is not just practical and aesthetically pleasing, but also morally and ethically sound and incredibly compassionate.

This journey demonstrates the potential for fusing spiritual insights with useful design abilities to create a harmonious balance that raises the role and standard of UX design in the digital era.

2.2 Navigating Controversies in Convergence

The ambitious and thought-provoking strategy of combining Buddhist philosophy with UX design takes us through a terrain full of contrasts and intellectual obstacles. This section of our journey explores the complex dance that exists between the calm, traditional teachings of Buddhism and the fast-paced, technologically advanced field of UX.

This is a road where the deep, spiritual wisdom passed down through the years collides with the state-of-the-art inventions of the digital world. This special combination creates a fusion that is complicated and intellectually engaging, characterized by a number of paradoxes and disputes that serve as doors rather than walls to greater comprehension and deeper insight. These contrasts challenge us to think critically, to push the boundaries of UX design, to look outside its traditional boundaries, and to consider how old philosophical principles might expand and enhance the field.

Every stage of this convergence trip explores the conflicts that naturally develop when cutting-edge technology and ageless spirituality collide. On the one hand, there is the dynamic, quickly changing field of user experience design, which is fueled by the need for ongoing innovation and adaptability to the constantly shifting needs of users and the development of technology. The constant pursuit of effectiveness, usefulness, and user happiness characterizes this world.

Conversely, we come across the contemplative and meditative tenets of Buddhism, a worldview that values self-reflection, moral behavior, and a profound comprehension of both the self and the cosmos.

The meeting point of these two domains, where the slow, deliberative, and contemplative ethos of Buddhist philosophy meets the instant satisfaction and solution-focused techniques of UX design, produces an intriguing interplay of ideas and approaches.

Maintaining a delicate balance and being open to complexity is necessary to successfully navigate this complicated terrain of contrasts and paradoxes. It pushes us to reevaluate the fundamentals of design and reinvent the meaning of creating digital experiences with ethical and spiritual considerations.

These debates require a rethinking of our responsibilities as designers and producers in the digital age; they are not merely theoretical exercises. They implore us to figure out how to combine the moral mindfulness and compassion of Buddhist teachings with the inventiveness and efficiency of UX design.

By doing this, we give ourselves access to a broader, more comprehensive approach to design — one that takes into account not just the short-term requirements of users but also the long-term effects on both their lives and the wider environment.

The purpose of this perpetual research is to understand and embrace the value that contradictions provide to our profession and our understanding of the digital experience, rather than to solve every one of them. It is a journey of constant learning, adaptation, and progress.

The Dilemma of Attachment and Detachment

We come across a deep and difficult conundrum: the conflict between the non-attachment philosophy of Buddhism and the objective of developing immersive, captivating user experiences.

At its core, user experience (UX) design aims to captivate users by creating interfaces and experiences that are both so natural and satisfying that they strengthen the bond between the user and the product. The underlying Buddhist concept of detachment, however, stands in stark contrast to the inherent goal of UX, which is to create this link and integrate digital experiences into the user's everyday life.

In order to attain enlightenment and inner peace, Buddhism emphasizes the importance of letting go of worldly attachments and promotes living a life that minimizes attachments to material possessions and fleeting experiences.

The design process becomes a difficult balancing act as a result of this juxtaposition.

- The difficulty is in developing captivating and engaging digital experiences without encouraging undue dependence or connection.
- Finding a careful balance that encourages user interaction without going too far in the direction of addictive behavior is key.
- This is making a deliberate effort to provide rewarding and meaningful experiences that simultaneously promote a positive relationship with technology.
- Aiming to fit with the Buddhist worldview, which encourages a detachment from an excessive dependence on any external source for happiness or fulfillment, the goal is to design interfaces and experiences that enrich users' lives without taking over as the center of their existence.

It takes a sophisticated grasp of human psychology as well as the more profound philosophical foundations of non-attachment to successfully navigate this conundrum. It demands a design philosophy that is both thoroughly conscious of the ethical consequences of digital products on users' lives and sympathetic and user-centric.

Rather than detracting from the design's quality or efficacy, this method enhances it by guaranteeing that the solutions we develop make a beneficial impact on users' lives without encouraging reliance.

This is one way that the fusion of non-attachment Buddhism and UX design provides a chance to rethink the place of digital encounters in our lives. It pushes us to design things that are not simply useful and beautiful to look at but also considerate of encouraging a good, balanced relationship with technology, in line with a more comprehensive vision of well-being and conscious living.

Ethical Design in a Profit-Driven World

The intersection of ethical design principles and the profit-driven motivations that frequently drive the technology industry gives rise to a crucial area of contention. Buddhism's teachings, which place a strong focus on mindfulness, compassion, and moral behavior, go against the traditional corporate mindset that places profit above all else.

> This poses important concerns for technologists and designers: How can we include compassion and ethical considerations in our solutions in a market that prioritizes financial success and competition? How do we make sure that our inventions uphold principles that advance the welfare of users and society at large, in addition to being commercially successful and making a positive contribution to the greater good?

This contradiction necessitates a thorough reconsideration of what success in the design industry really means. *It advocates for a change in mindset from seeing success only in terms of financial profitability to taking a more all-*

encompassing approach that prioritizes user welfare, ethical integrity, and societal influence.

This change is more than simply a theoretical ideal; it necessitates realigning our approaches to design and success measurement with practical solutions. It involves developing design strategies that balance business goals with moral principles, making sure that our creations are not just aesthetically pleasing and marketable but also socially conscious and uphold a higher ethical standard.

This reassessment of design success measures pushes us to consider novel approaches for producing designs that are not only profitable but also benefit users and society as a whole; designs that are not just consumer software but agents of positive change.

In order to successfully navigate this complicated landscape, one must strike a careful balance between the pursuit of wealth and a dedication to morality and social duty. It entails developing a design philosophy that acknowledges both the significant influence that profit has on the sustainability of businesses and the users of this work, as well as the global impact of such creations.

> We can develop experiences and products that connect with people more deeply by including the ideals of compassion and mindfulness into the design process. This will promote trust and loyalty among users and move technology toward a more moral and conscious use.

This design methodology not only helps firms become more credible and well-known, but it also makes the IT industry fairer and more conscientious. *By working with this mindset, we are doing more than just designing for the current market; we are influencing technology's direction and bringing innovation and morality together to create a digital environment that is not just profitable but also morally and empathetic.*

A Path Forward

These complexities are not obstacles but rather essential parts of our path, providing chances for deep development and comprehension. To successfully traverse this route, one must embrace these tensions. It entails understanding that these seemingly incompatible ideas can really promote a more holistic, compassionate, and ethically sensitive method of design.

Continuous questioning, learning, and adaptation characterize this process, which is essentially dynamic. Staying open to fresh discoveries, viewpoints, and understandings is more important than finding ultimate solutions to these contradictions. Because of this transparency, we are able to improve our design process and help create a more considerate, caring, and morally sound digital environment.

Exploring the intersection of user experience design and Buddhist philosophy forces us to question established norms in the field. To think about how our products will affect people's lives and the world at large is a challenge it poses.

Insights gained from this investigation lead us to believe that design is about more than just making good digital products; it can also help us forge stronger bonds between technology and our everyday lives.

In a future where technology is both useful and aligned with human existence's higher values, we can bridge the gap between UX design's practical abilities and Buddhism's deep ethical and philosophical insights.

> Following this road will allow us to build digital experiences that are revolutionary, interesting, and engaging, but also caring and enriching people's lives, experiences that speak to people's innermost desires and help society thrive.

Embracing these debates and conflicts demonstrates the revolutionary potential of merging pragmatic design knowledge with profound philosophical insight. It represents a shift towards a more comprehensive view of technology, where compassion and innovation coexist, mindfulness and efficiency coexist, and financial success coexists with moral obligation.

The goal of this holistic strategy is to influence how people will use technology in the future, not merely to create software portals and user-centric products. It is an adventure that changes the designer's function from making digital interfaces to helping people have meaningful experiences.

Along this path, we are not merely adding to technology's development; we are molding it into a digital world that is more aware, ethical, and compassionate, one in which spirituality and technology live in perfect harmony to improve and elevate human life.

Designing
with Insight

DELVING INTO WISDOM

This part invites us to delve deeper into the rich tapestry of *insight* that arises from the synthesis of the contemplative and enlightened teachings of Buddhism with the real-world application of user experience design. *Here, we are not merely artists or designers; rather, we are sages, delving into the depths of comprehension and perception that this special amalgamation provides.*

In this investigation, we go into the domains of increased consciousness and understanding, discovering how the Buddhist precepts might provide light on the UX design process. This journey is about changing the fundamental principles of how we approach the production of digital experiences, not just about applying Buddhist beliefs to design. We step into a realm where design is no longer limited by convention, where designing digital interfaces is an ethical, thoughtful, and aware endeavor.

It is our invitation to view our work with a more compassionate and profound perspective. It pushes us to consider why we design as well as how we design. We will examine how ethical considerations can direct us toward more responsible and advantageous digital products, how incorporating mindfulness into the design process can result in more intuitive and empathic user experiences, and how the pursuit of wisdom in design can result in more meaningful and enriching digital interactions in this section.

> This road leads to a more perceptive, deliberate, and enlightened approach to UX design; it is a path where every action is done mindfully, every choice is made with the larger good in mind, and every product is given a stronger sense of meaning.

As we proceed through this portion, we welcome the wisdom that arises from this special synthesis and allow it to inform our decisions, deeds, and artistic endeavors. "Designing with Insight" is more than just a chapter in a book; it is an exploration of the essence of conscious and purposeful creation that has the power to change not just our designs but also ourselves as artists and people.

CHAPTER 3

Pervading Wisdom: Designing with Right View

3.1 User-Centered Insight: Amplifying Empathy

Right View is a fundamental idea that greatly influences our way of designing user experiences and is at the heart of the blending of UX design with Buddhist philosophy.

Within the field of user experience, *Right View refers to a viewpoint that prioritizes the requirements, feelings, and experiences of the user throughout the design process, demonstrating a profound empathy for consumers.*

In design, empathy goes beyond a cursory grasp of the user; it entails:

- entering their world,
- experiencing it through their eyes,
- even through their mouse and keyboard,
- and connecting with them on an emotional level.

A digital experience that connects emotionally and resonates deeply with the user's underlying needs and ambitions is the result of using an empathic approach.

Building on this idea, we investigate how empathy may be a useful tool for producing more significant and memorable user experiences when it is truly incorporated into UX design. It entails a change in perspective from considering design as a technical undertaking to considering it as a means of communicating empathy.

This change necessitates a thorough comprehension of the user — not just as the final consumer of a good or service — as a whole. We may start designing solutions that are both emotionally intelligent and user-friendly by incorporating empathy into the design process. These designs consider the nuances of human emotion and thought, resulting in intuitive, captivating, and deeply fulfilling experiences.

Because it encourages a more responsible and caring relationship with the user and prioritizes their well-being as a crucial component of the design outcome, this empathetic approach also adds an ethical dimension to design.

> Furthermore, empathy in UX design forces us to continuously improve our comprehension of the user, maintain new ideas, and maintain an open mind. It is a dynamic process that calls for constant learning, hearing, and adjustment. By adopting empathy, we pledge to have a design approach that is dynamic and adaptable to the users' changing demands and environments.

This method not only improves the caliber and applicability of our designs, but it also unites our efforts with a more profound feeling of meaning and purpose. *Essentially, incorporating empathy into UX design is about more than just making user experiences better — it is about changing the way we interact with our users and building a compassionate and understanding bridge that enhances both our products and our roles as designers.*

The Lens of Compassion in UX

Examining the domains of UX design via the sympathetic prism of empathy fundamentally alters how we create digital experiences. This greater empathy goes far beyond a surface-level comprehension of user needs; rather, it is an immersive voyage into the user's emotional world, where their joys, frustrations, and problems are not just witnessed but also intensely felt and experienced.

By integrating compassion at the center of the design process, this empathic approach goes beyond conventional design paradigms:

- The experiences and products we build take on new dimensions when empathy is the cornerstone of our design thinking.
- They are not only attractive and useful, but also precisely tailored to the subtleties of the human experience.
- This enhanced methodology cultivates a design process that is not only intuitive and responsive but also deeply human-centered,
- resulting in the development of digital experiences that transcend screen interactions to create authentic, significant connections.

In order to effectively engage with customers' emotional landscapes and comprehend their experiences from a position of profound empathy, UX designers must adopt a compassionate lens. Through the meticulous consideration and respect of each user's story, this approach turns the design process into a human experience narrative.

Within this framework, empathy serves as a tool to help designers create designs that are companions in the user's everyday life as well as problem-solving tools. Empathically designed digital experiences strike a more personal chord with consumers, offering comfort, empathy, and a sense of connection in addition to a service or functionality.

Products that satisfy users' functional needs, as well as their emotional and psychological needs, are the result of this transition towards a more compassionate approach to

UX design, resulting in a seamless fusion of technology and humanity.

Additionally, *the use of compassion in UX design enhances the position of the designer by changing it from one of a creator to one of an understanding collaborator in the user's journey.* This increased responsibility forces designers to have a thorough understanding of how their work affects consumers' emotional and psychological states.

It demands a deliberate process where each design choice is considered carefully, taking into account not just the practical and aesthetic effects but also the ethical and emotional resonance of the choice. In this sense, including empathy into UX design opens the door to the development of digital products that are more sympathetic and empathetic.

Through a journey where the boundaries between technology and human experience are blurred, and design is elevated to a sort of sympathetic craftsmanship, digital products are created that are not merely used but felt and lived. This humane approach to UX design opens the door to a world where digital encounters are deeply nourishing, compassionate, and related to the human spirit in addition to being effective and entertaining.

Ethical Implications of Empathetic Design

As we incorporate the deep component of empathy into UX design, we naturally enter a more expansive ethical domain. *Enhancing empathy in the design process entails a duty that transcends technical mastery and visual attractiveness.*

It entails making thoughtful decisions that prioritize the welfare of the user over the traditional emphasis on utility and aesthetic design. A more thorough examination of the ways in which our designs affect users' mental and emotional well-being is required by this ethical viewpoint.

> Conscience-driven design is carefully evaluating each component, feature, and interaction for how it might impact the user's mental health and quality of life in general. Using this method elevates the user experience from simply user-friendly to truly life-enhancing, making empathic design a potent force for good.

This move toward ethically grounded, empathic design necessitates a comprehensive reassessment of our design tactics and priorities. It pushes us to give users' privacy, liberty, and a sense of dignity-first priority at every step of the design process.

This entails developing digital experiences that support users' long-term well-being in addition to meeting their current requirements. It involves designing user interfaces and interactions with consideration for the user's personal boundaries, mental health, and empowerment. This ethical component makes sure that our ideas make a meaningful and positive impact on the lives of users, supporting the notion that excellent design is about compassion, respect, and ethical duty in addition to efficiency and engagement.

> Accepting the moral ramifications of empathic design involves a fundamental change in design philosophy rather than just a procedural stage in the process. It is a call to action for designers to embrace empathy as a fundamental tenet of their work, rather than just as a tool.

We discover that adopting an empathic UX design approach fosters a more meaningful and profound relationship with our users as we progress along its route. *It is a bond that reaches deep into the human spirit, beyond the confines of the digital interface.*

We are always learning, growing, and redefining our role as designers on this journey. It motivates us to design digital experiences that are not only visually beautiful and technically sound, but also deeply human, moral, and compassionate. By taking this route, we help to create experiences that not only fulfill users' functional demands but also enhance their lives and preserve their humanity and dignity. In short, we help to shape a digital world that genuinely revolves around the user in the fullest, most sympathetic sense.

3.2 Holistic Perspective: The Buddha's Right View in Design

Stepping upon the creative path of fusing Buddhist teachings with UX design, we come across the profound notion of *Right View* as a fundamental tenet. In Buddhism, *Right View* refers to a perception of reality that is free from errors or misconceptions, one that is correct and clear. When integrated into UX design, this idea develops into a comprehensive strategy that goes beyond traditional user needs assessments. This integration signals a change in focus from only taking care of the needs and features on the surface to interacting with the richer, more complex fabric of the user's life and experiences.

It is about viewing the user's world as a dynamic interplay of emotions, environments, and interactions rather than a static set of criteria. With this viewpoint, designers can go beyond what is immediately visible and evaluate how their work fits into the larger story of the user's life, which may impact their experiences and well-being.

Right View adoption in UX design encourages a more in-depth, compassionate interaction with users. It is about developing a comprehension that explores the full human experience, going beyond user profiles and analytics.

This method considers the user's concerns and goals as well as their emotional landscape, cultural background, and social situation. Incorporating *Right View* means that designers are developing for a person, a complex and multifaceted entity, rather than just a user.

This all-encompassing approach results in the production of experiences and goods that have a deeper resonance, establishing a lasting and meaningful relationship. It is a design philosophy that acknowledges that every design choice has repercussions that go well beyond the digital interface and sees the user as an essential component of a bigger ecosystem.

Adding *Right View* into UX design also gives the process a special ethical component. It involves taking into account the ethical ramifications of each feature, interaction, and experience while designing with a conscience that respects the autonomy and dignity of the user.

This thoughtful approach guarantees that designs support a harmonic balance between personal well-being and technology use, not only by fulfilling practical requirements but also by favorably impacting the mental and emotional health of the user. *Right View* becomes more than just a design guideline in this way; it becomes a beacon of light for moral and humanitarian UX practices, resulting in the development of digital experiences that are not just effective and user-friendly but also nurturing and enriching of life.

Buddhist philosophy serves as the inspiration for this holistic approach to UX design, which opens the door to a future in which technology meets not just our practical requirements but also our more fundamental human desires for ethical interaction, connection, and understanding.

Beyond Functionality: Understanding the User's World

Taking a *Right View* approach to UX design allows us to see the user's world from a wider, more linked perspective. This viewpoint goes beyond the conventional understanding of users as merely technology consumers to see them as multifaceted people leading varied and full lives.

This holistic approach views the user as a whole person with a distinct tapestry of emotions, experiences, and goals, rather than only in the context of their encounter with a digital product. This change in viewpoint forces us to think about every aspect of the user's life and comprehend how our designs integrate into and influence their larger life story. It is an approach that forces us to think about a product's involvement in the user's total well-being rather than just its immediate utility.

> When designing using this *Right View* perspective, one must interact with the user's world as a whole. It entails delving deeply into an awareness of their surroundings, social dynamics, cultural background, emotional terrain, and immediate needs and desires.

By taking a holistic approach, we can create experiences that are not just operationally pleasing but also emotionally and psychologically rewarding for the consumer, enabling us to develop things that resonate more profoundly with them. It is about understanding how our design choices affect the user's life and how each feature, interaction, and interface may influence the user's mental and emotional health. By keeping this in mind when we create, we make sure that our products serve as companions along the way, supporting the user's goals and ideals while also improving their quality of life overall.

Right View becomes a guiding concept in this context, helping designers create designs that are more responsible, compassionate, and user focused. It inspires us to design experiences that are genuinely user-centered, attentive, and thoughtful. This method helps create a more compassionate and ethical digital environment in addition to improving the user experience in a functional sense. We go beyond simple functionality by taking into account the user's reality as a whole and developing with their holistic needs in mind.

> We enter a realm where design is about more than just making effective user interfaces; it is about enhancing people's lives, generating happy experiences, and improving our users' general well-being. Embracing *Right View* in UX design so becomes an essential component of a greater goal: to build a digital world that is truly human, thoughtful, and life-affirming, in addition to being technologically sophisticated.

Ethical Mindfulness in Design Decisions

Rethinking our fundamental function as designers is at the heart of this change, which goes beyond merely improving the design process. Adopting this viewpoint compels us to operate more responsibly, thinking about the bigger picture of the ethical consequences of our design decisions.

What this implies is that we need to ask more meaningful questions, ones that go beyond simple concerns about form and function:

- In what ways do our designs affect how people engage with digital tools?
- Are we designing experiences that value the user's privacy, focus, and time?
- Are we making things worse for them or better for them in general?

Digital experiences must adhere to technical and usability criteria while also respecting the user's dignity, autonomy, and welfare if we are to incorporate *Right View* into our design philosophy.

More empathy and focus on people's need result from making design decisions with this ethical mindfulness. It is a way of thinking about design that considers every project as a chance to make a positive difference in the user's life, whether it is through practicality, ethics, or emotion.

> It is important to remember that as designers we have the capacity to shape experiences, influence behaviors, and impact lives. This perspective reminds us of this power. We make sure our designs do more than just fix problems; we make sure they improve people's lives by encouraging a better and more considerate relationship with technology by keeping the ethical aspects of our job in mind.

This moral perspective on user experience design transforms the field from a job focused on getting things done to a vocation that is actively involved in making the world a better place.

Embracing ethical consciousness in design is a continuous and ever-changing endeavor. It forces us to think about the ethical implications of our work constantly, to learn more about the user's needs, and to create designs that are good for the world and the people in it.

We help build a more equitable and caring digital world by incorporating *Right View* into our design philosophy. By taking this tactic, we can improve the user experience and establish design as a powerful force for creating a tech world that is more compassionate, ethical, and thoughtful. With *Right View*, we channel the power that comes with being designers into making digital experiences that are superior in terms of functionality, but also more fulfilling in terms of ethics and holistically human.

CHAPTER 4

Ethical Intentions: Designing with Right Intention

4.1 Shaping Ethical Foundations: Intentions in UX

An integral part of the Eightfold Path, the concept of *Right Intention*, is crucial to the novel integration of user experience design with Buddhist teachings.

This chapter delves into the impact of *Right Intention* on the foundation of UX design's ethical principles. *Right Intention* within this framework encourages a practice based on ethical consciousness and selfless motivations, moving beyond the conventional design goals.

This method emphasizes the need to coordinate our design efforts with values that are both ethical and socially aware, in addition to being technically competent. This requires a dedication to designing with users' health and worth in mind, making sure our creations improve people's lives and the world at large in addition to serving their practical needs.

Right Intention is the beacon that illuminates this method, prompting us to reevaluate and reshape our reasons for being involved in the design process altogether. It stresses the need to think about how our efforts will affect the world at large:

- Do we want our designs to make a difference in people's lives?
- Is the inherent worth and freedom of every person honored and protected?

We begin to perceive our position as builders of experiences that enrich and uplift, rather than merely creators of visually beautiful and useful interfaces, when we incorporate Right Intention into our UX methods.

By adopting this outlook, we move our attention from meeting short-term user demands to cultivating enjoyment and well-being in the long run. It is a paradigm shift that makes what we do more than just technical execution; it is a practice that is both compassionate and ethical.

We may form a stronger bond with our work and our users by adhering to the *Right Intention* principle in user experience design. By considering the effects on people and communities both now and in the future, it turns the design process into an ethical exploration.

Products that are both creative and easy to use, but also supportive and empowering, are what we aim for when we utilize this thoughtful approach to design. This motivates us to create digital experiences that truly connect with users, earning their trust and loyalty by showing that we care about them and value them.

Right Intention is a step in the right direction toward a future where user experience design is about more than just making good interfaces; it is about making our created internet a better, more caring, and more ethical place for everyone.

Ethical Intentions: Beyond Aesthetics and Functionality

The incorporation of *Right Intention* into UX design is a sea of change in our methodology. It implies that a strong feeling of ethical duty and a determination to make a positive influence should permeate the entire design process, from the first ideation to the final implementation.

This paradigm shifts our focus from purely practical and aesthetically pleasing designs to ones that prioritize ethical considerations. In this area, we no longer limit our decision-making to meeting the user's immediate wants and needs or to accomplishing corporate goals in isolation.

Rather, they take on a higher mission:

- to prioritize the user's mental and emotional health,
- to safeguard their privacy,
- and to empower them to make their own decisions.

Our *Right Intention* design philosophy helps us to reevaluate our position as designers. Our work goes beyond making goods that look attractive and work well; it also serves as a vehicle for doing good in the world.

From this vantage point, we cannot help but wonder how our design decisions will play out in the grand scheme of things:

- Is our presence adding to the din of negative online encounters or helping to foster a culture of healthy online interactions?
- Is the user experience we are creating giving them more control, or are we unintentionally making them more dependent?

We put *Right Intention* first in our design process so that we may make things that are beautiful and functional and that improve people's lives and society as a whole.

> *Right Intention* is more than just a methodology in user experience design; it is a moral compass that points us in the direction of more caring and accountable actions. It encourages us to see every project as a chance to make a difference in the world, improving user experiences one step at a time.

With this method, we can make digital goods and experiences that touch people's lives in meaningful ways, not only via their practicality and aesthetics, but also through the principles they stand for and the progress they encourage. By incorporating *Right Intention* into our work, we aim to create experiences that are not only functional and entertaining, but also meet ethical standards, provide psychological support, and contribute to society in a meaningful way. *This will redefine the role of the designer in the digital era.*

The Role of Intentions in Shaping User Experience

There has been a sea change in our approach to design thinking and practice since we incorporated the principle of *Right Intention,* which originates in Buddhist philosophy. This emphasis on *Right Intention* signals a more caring and accountable method of design, taking our job beyond simple screen-based interactions and into experiences that deeply affect users' lives.

From this vantage point, we should think about how our designs will affect people in due course, not just how they will look and work right now. The focus should be on making experiences that go beyond just satisfying the user and instead go the extra mile to help them grow and thrive. We build a stronger bond with our customers and the digital products we make for them by following this moral compass. *As time goes on, users begin to notice and cherish the design's well-considered and respectful approach to their well-being and values.*

We infuse our work with a feeling of purpose and ethical responsibility through our commitment to *Right Intention* in design. By including users' mental, emotional, and spiritual health, it elevates design to a more holistic profession.

The design process becomes more than just a technical exercise; it becomes a moral and empathic journey where every option reflects our aim to help and enrich the user's life. Experiences that are not only practical but also touching, morally upright, and profoundly humanizing are born from this method. By putting an emphasis on *Right Intention*, we are able to coordinate our efforts with the overarching objective of making digital spaces that promote the development and flourishing of their users.

By incorporating *Right Intention* into user experience design, we can revolutionize the way technology affects our lives. Designers should see their job as a chance to improve people's lives, not simply how they act but also the quality of their daily lives in general.

To make sure our designs are both technically sound, morally sound, and useful, we must continually assess and improve our intentions in light of this principle, which we have incorporated into our design philosophy. *Right Intention* goes beyond being a design guideline and instead becomes a guiding force that influences the entire user experience, from ideation to the finished product.

4.2 Buddhist Ethical Design: Aligning with User Values

Buddhism provides a rich ethical framework that can inform and influence our design techniques; this framework is based on compassion, mindfulness, and respect for all life. Rather than being an afterthought, the incorporation of Buddhist ethical concepts into our designs constitutes a radical shift in our methodology.

Making digital products that speak to people's values and principles, as well as their practical and technological needs, is what this is all about. This moral undercurrent compels us to think about how our goods might represent and support principles like responsibility, empathy, and kindness, in addition to their practicality and aesthetic appeal.

In this method, we base our design decisions on Buddhist principles, which remind us to consider the user as a whole. It entails making a deliberate attempt to guarantee that our digital works are more than just resources; they are also channels for constructive ethical participation.

From this vantage point, we can see the bigger picture of designing with the common good in mind, rather than narrowly focused on user happiness and financial gain. Starting with how each aspect, interaction, and functionality adds to the user's well-being and how they connect with the principles of ethical living, we begin to analyze every design decision through the lens of ethical effect.

We set out to build digital solutions that do more than just meet users' functional needs; we want to help them on their ethical and spiritual path by incorporating Buddhist ideals into our design philosophy.

More caring and accountable work results from applying Buddhist ethical concepts to user experience design. As a result, we need to think carefully about how our work will affect others and the world around us if we want to design digital experiences that are good for people and the planet.

This method promotes a culture of empathy and mindfulness in design, which in turn encourages designers to think about the bigger picture when they make something.

By incorporating Buddhist ethics into user experience design, we may create digital technology that is not just cutting-edge and focused on users, but also ethically aware and in harmony with humankind's highest ideals and principles. It is a path that reimagines what it means to design, with user values and ethical concerns serving as the foundation for creating experiences that matter.

Designing for a Harmonious User Experience

Now, it is all about making digital experiences that align with user values and enhance their entire quality of life. By going beyond surface-level considerations of form and function, this method probes the more profound effects of our design decisions on consumers' moral and psychological health.

It is a way of thinking about design that takes it beyond just making things easier for people to use and instead aims to promote unity, dignity, and moral integrity. The goal of this design phi-losophy is to create goods that not only serve consumers' functional demands but also speak to their sense of right and wrong. By harmonizing our efforts in this way, we can guarantee that the goods we make will become indispensable parts of our customers' lives, rather than merely means of interaction.

The incorporation of Buddhist ethical concepts into user experience design prompts us to think about how our work will affect the user in the long run. A well-rounded and satisfying user experience is the result of meticulous con-sideration of how every aspect of the design, interaction, and feature works together.

By incorporating ethical and value-based concerns into the design process from the start, we can make sure that our products serve their intended purpose while also mak-ing people feel good about themselves. We can create dig-ital experiences that are powerful and nurturing by making harmony and ethical integrity our top design priorities. These experiences will support the user's emotional health and help them on their path to a fulfilled existence.

There has been a sea change in our perspective as de-signers with the move toward creating digital experiences that are harmonious. It pushes us to consider the user's life from a deeper perspective, going beyond the obvious ways our designs connect with them. This viewpoint encourages a more meaningful relationship between the user and the digital product, one that is based on mutual regard and comprehension.

By considering users' moral and psychological demands when we design, we help build a digital world that is responsive, caring, and in line with humanity's larger goals, not to mention efficient and easy to use. Thus, by prioritizing a balanced user experience, we may build digital goods that are cutting edge in terms of technology, but also kind, considerate, and ethically beneficial, elevating the digital age human condition.

Upholding Ethical Standards in the Digital Realm

Incorporating Buddhist ethical concepts into user experience design serves as a powerful reminder to designers to always behave with integrity. This dedication goes beyond just being innovative and easy to use; it also covers areas like social responsibility and having high ethical standards. It entails thinking about the bigger picture when we create, keeping in mind the social and environmental impacts of our work.

This view necessitates thinking about how our ideas will affect people and the world in the long run, in addition to how they will affect users in the short term. We commit to making digital goods and experiences that are naturally kind and considerate by incorporating Buddhist ideals into UX design. We will not abuse, deceive, or hurt people or the environment in any way.

In order to make a positive impact on the world, we want to find answers that address current problems while also being in line with sustainable and ethical lifestyle values.

> This moral stance in user experience design is all about rethinking how technology will change our lives. It asks us to think about how our innovations can benefit society as a whole, rather than just improving technology for the sake of it.

In this view, an ethical consciousness permeates the whole design process, from initial ideation to final execution. It is all about making digital products that are beautiful and practical, but also built on principles of kindness, awareness, and reverence for all living things. This moral component adds nuance to the design process, pushing us toward actions that are good for society and the environment in addition to being creatively fulfilling.

As such, it marks the beginning of a new age in which design serves as a vehicle for advocating for social and ethical well-being as well as user interfaces. Buddhist ethics are not merely a set of rules to follow; they are the bedrock principles upon which our creative work is based.

This change signifies a more comprehensive rethinking of what it means to be successful as a designer. We are now considering not only how well our work works technically and how engaged people are, but also how well it aligns with their underlying values and whether it has ethical merit. *Through the adoption of this approach, we can help shape a digital world that is more ethical, compassionate, and focused on values.*

In this world, technology should not only meet our immediate needs but also contribute to humanity's higher ambitions, allowing us to create experiences that are effective, interactive, respectful, and morally sound.

SECTION 3

The Path Unveiled

JOURNEYING INTO TRANSFORMATION

Stepping into Section III, *The Path Unveiled*, we go further into the life-altering adventure where user experience design meets the deep knowledge of Buddhism. Here we shed light on how to include ethical and mindful practices into our design processes from the ground up, which will lead to profound changes for the designer and the user alike. In this article, we delve into how the teachings of

Buddhism illuminate our creative function in the digital realm and improve our design process.

Join me on a captivating trip through *The Path Unveiled* as we delve into the profound impact of Buddhist teachings on the field of user experience design. It is about going above and above with a holistic approach that combines mindfulness with practicality, compassion with efficiency, and innovation with moral honesty, rather than relying on conventional design techniques.

> As we go further into this part, we will examine the different aspects of this integration, such as making designs that do more than just fix problems; they also encourage personal growth and wellness. We will also construct digital experiences that are deeply human-centric — rather than just user-centric.

Along this path of metamorphosis, we are not merely seeking to hone our design abilities, but also to broaden our worldview and method of approaching the field. This is the road that pushes us to contemplate the bigger picture, how our inventions will affect people and the world at large, rather than just the narrow focus of our jobs.

We welcome the chance to design a future where spirituality and technology merge as we make our way along *The Path Unveiled*, with the goal of making digital experiences that are both technologically advanced and spiritually enriching. *A call to designers and makers in this part of the book to enter the world of mindful design, where every action is a step toward making the digital world more kind, honest, and wise.*

CHAPTER 5

Impactful Design: Creating with Right Action

5.1 Guiding Design with UX Ethics: Right Action

Right Action is a cornerstone idea that emerges in the complex intersection of UX design and Buddhist philosophy. It has a tremendous impact on the ethical landscape of design. Incorporating the tenet of *Right Action*, central to the Eightfold Path of the Buddha, into the principles of user experience design has a profound effect, as this chapter explains. *Right Action* is a beacon that designers can follow in this regard, leading them to methods that are ethical and socially responsible in addition to being good at satisfying user demands.

Right Action in user experience design boils down to purposefully making choices and implementing tactics that benefit user experience and society at large. The focus should be on how these decisions align with ethical ideals and impact communal well-being rather than only on their utility and attractiveness.

The *Right Action* methodology for user experience design entails doing things the right way. Designing with users' different requirements and circumstances in mind requires a strong dedication to making designs that are accessible, inclusive, and welcoming.

As part of this dedication, we will not rest until we guarantee that our designs promote inclusion and strength rather than oppression. In addition, the concept of *Right Action* in design suggests an obligation to safeguard user data and identity by making trustworthy and transparent digital goods.

> Integrating integrity and moral reasoning into the design process from the very beginning, during user research, all the way to the end, during product deployment and feedback, is the goal.

We begin our path toward ethical transformation by including *Right Action* in user experience design. This method encourages us to think about and assess the moral consequences of our actions in a constant loop, with the goal of making goods that do more than just meet needs; they should also improve people's lives and empower communities.

> Along the way, we will need to strike a balance between being innovative and being cognizant of our ethical responsibilities; we must strive to innovate in ways that are both technologically sophisticated and socially responsible.

Embracing *Right Action* helps usher in a new era of user experience design, where ethical consciousness is integral to the creative process. This will result in digital experiences that are not only focused on the user, but also incredibly compassionate and morally beneficial.

Principles of Right Action in Design

Adopting the *Right Action* principles results in a multidimensional strategy that has a significant impact on how we develop and execute our projects. *Right Action* is fundamentally about having a strong commitment to integrity and openness.

As part of this ethical position, we make sure that our designs are clear, honest, devoid of any kind of deception or misdirection, as well as aesthetically beautiful and robust in terms of functionality. This kind of dedication is essential to building people's trust and confidence and ensuring that they can depend on our products for both their usefulness and their integrity. Moreover, this concept encompasses safeguarding user confidentiality and information, an essential facet in the contemporary digital environment. Respecting user autonomy and personal space in the digital sphere by protecting user privacy is not only legally required but also morally required.

Furthermore, the design concept of *Right Action* includes the careful avoidance of harm. This element necessitates that we designers be highly conscious of any potential drawbacks that our designs may have. It entails taking a proactive stance to anticipate and address problems like user addiction, the dissemination of false information, or the unintentional perpetuation of damaging preconceptions and biases.

> It is our duty to make sure that our designs improve both the lives of the users and the larger social fabric, doing more good than harm. In order to do this, we work hard to produce designs that enhance well-being, empathy, and constructive behavior in addition to providing solutions to issues. A meticulous balancing act is required here, with each feature, interaction, and piece of material being carefully considered for any potential long- and short-term effects.

By embracing the *Right Action* principles, we pledge to employ a design process that is not just highly skilled and user-focused but also morally and socially responsible. It is a comprehensive method that takes into account the broader effects of our design decisions and how they affect the user's mental, emotional, and physical well-being. With this method, the design process becomes a thoughtful activity in which every choice we make is a reflection of our moral values and our commitment to creating good in the world through our work.

By integrating the *Right Action* tenets into our designs, we help create a digital world that is more moral, responsible, and caring — one in which technology fulfills not just the necessities but also the greatest hopes and dreams of humanity.

Implementing Right Action in Design Processes

Right Action, as a component of the UX design process, represents a paradigm change in how we approach creativity on all fronts. This change is about incorporating a mindset of doing good and acting responsibly into every step of the creative process, not just about following ethical guidelines.

Right Action is a compass that directs our decisions and actions from the beginning, when ideas and concepts start to take shape, to the end, when testing and product launches are taking place. In order to apply this ethical approach, user research must be inclusive and sympathetic in order to reconcile respecting users' autonomy and dignity with knowing their needs and situation. It also applies to ideation and design, where inventiveness is combined with an awareness of the wider effects on people and communities.

Right Action demands that we continually assess and re-assess our work through an ethical lens as we move through the creative process. It involves being watchful and proactive in seeing the dangers or unfavorable effects of our ideas and acting to reduce them.

This entails being aware of the potential effects that our designs may have on user behavior, taking into account factors like inclusivity, privacy, and digital well-being. It entails developing designs that improve user quality of life and make a beneficial impact on community welfare in addition to solving problems. In actuality, this entails testing and improving our designs iteratively while getting input on social impact and ethical issues in addition to usability and functionality.

> Including *Right Action* in our design processes is a conceptual commitment to ethical consciousness rather than just a procedural modification. With this dedication, the designer becomes more than just a maker of digital goods — rather, a steward of ethical and kind technology.

By including *Right Action* as a fundamental principle, we guarantee that our designs are in compliance with the highest ethical standards while also improving their quality and efficacy. This methodology opens the door to the development of digital experiences that are not only creative and captivating but also socially and morally uplifting.

By choosing this course, we as designers actively contribute to the creation of a digital environment that values justice, compassion, and moral rectitude, transforming technology into a positive social force.

5.2 Aligning with User Values: The Ethical Foundations

Aligning our design processes with user values is an important endeavor in the complex fusion of UX design with Buddhist ethical principles. In order to achieve a profound alignment with users' moral and ethical beliefs, this chapter delves into the dynamic interplay between *Right Action*, a fundamental component of the Buddha's Eightfold Path, and its application in UX design.

Designing with *Right Action* in mind entails deeply integrating users' moral and ethical choices into every facet of the design process, going beyond simple usefulness and aesthetics. This method broadens the scope of conventional UX paradigms by emphasizing moral issues, including user privacy, equity, inclusion, and environmental sustainability. We create digital solutions that speak to users' deeper ethical convictions and ideals in addition to their practical demands by emphasizing these ethical elements in our design process.

This dedication to ethical integration calls for a sophisticated comprehension of the various values and beliefs held by our users:

- It starts with a rigorous and compassionate research procedure that gathers and analyzes user perspectives on ethics with the same level of rigor as functional requirements.

- It involves listening intently, posing pertinent questions, and comprehending the intricate web of values that shapes how people engage with technology.
- In order to ensure that users' voices and beliefs are not only heard but also have a significant influence on the final product, this understanding process also involves actively involving users in the design process.
- In this sense, the design process turns into a co-operative undertaking in which ethical issues are assiduously integrated into the overall concept from the outset.

By incorporating *Right Action* into UX design, we also take on the duty of always choosing morally. This entails creating with a keen understanding of how our decisions affect the larger social and environmental context in addition to the user experience. It entails making thoughtful choices that protect user privacy, guarantee equity and accessibility, and take sustainability into account for our designs. Designing with an ethical consciousness results in digital goods that are not only effective and entertaining, but also ethically upright and demonstrate a profound regard for the values and welfare of its users.

To sum up, including ethical issues into user-centric design is a commitment to enhancing the role of design in society rather than just a tactical move. We contribute to a digital environment that is deeply human, ethically rich, and technologically advanced by integrating user values into our designs.

Understanding and Integrating User Values

Within the field of user experience design, which is based on the *Right Action* principles, comprehending and incorporating user values becomes a crucial part of the design process. This trip thoroughly maps the ethical and moral terrain of the users, going beyond merely attending to functional needs and usability.

The approach starts with a comprehensive and immersive phase of user research, where the objective is to obtain a profound understanding of the users' ethical views and values in addition to identifying their practical demands and preferences.

Engaging with people to learn about their viewpoints on technology, underlying beliefs, and ethical expectations for digital products is part of this inquiry. It involves asking more in-depth, thoughtful questions that delve into the users' expectations of digital privacy, thoughts on the impact of technology on society, and attitudes about what constitutes ethical technology use.

This method of comprehending user values calls for a change in the role of the designer — from one of complex designers to one of sympathetic collaborators in the user's journey. It requires designers to engage with consumers in an open-minded and compassionate manner, listening carefully to fully comprehend and internalize the

> user's ethical perspective — rather than only re-
> sponding to problems or offering solutions.

This procedure frequently reveals a wide range of intricate ethical considerations and user values, from views re-
garding social justice and environmental sustainability to
worries about data security and privacy. Designers may
produce solutions that are both ethically and functionally
sound and in line with the ideals of the consumers by embracing this variety.

User values integration into UX design is a dynamic,
continuing process. It necessitates constant communication
with consumers in order to stay aware of their changing
ethical viewpoints and modify designs appropriately. It entails a dedication to producing designs that mirror users'
moral principles, making sure that the digital goods we develop are not only instruments for productivity but also living examples of the principles people cherish.

We open the door to developing digital experiences that
are not just efficient and captivating, but also strongly cor-
related with the moral and ethical fiber of the user's life by
placing a high priority on comprehending and incorporating user values into design. By sharing a dedication to
moral values, this alignment strengthens the bond between
the user and the product, fostering loyalty and trust.

Designing with Ethical Integrity

This methodology converts the design process into a deliberate journey in which every choice is closely considered
in light of its ethical implications. It is a change that gives

moral issues the same weight as practicality and visual appeal. In this situation, designers have an obligation to create experiences that are not just aesthetically pleasing and functional but also firmly based on moral principles and representative of the values of the users. This dedication to morality extends to several aspects of design, such as the interface's structure and data management guidelines.

To make sure the design complies with ethical norms, each component is carefully considered. This involves putting a lot of focus on accessibility to make sure that anyone can use digital products, regardless of background or ability. Data security and privacy are also critical, necessitating designs that secure user data and foster confidence.

Moreover, environmental concerns are a part of ethical integrity in design, which forces designers to evaluate the ecological implications and sustainability of their decisions. Designers must resolve difficult moral conundrums when tackling these issues, such as juggling the need for strict data security with user comfort or handling the complexities of getting actual user consent.

By adhering strictly to the *Right Action* principles and giving priority to alignment with user values, designers pave the way for the creation of digital experiences that are morally and ethically compelling. This paradigm change in design philosophy fosters a holistic approach where ethical issues are just as vital as practical and aesthetic features, going beyond traditional objectives.

Designers may help shape a digital environment that not only excels in technological innovation but also upholds and reflects the ethical values and higher goals of society by adopting this comprehensive approach. In this sense, driven by a strong dedication to moral integrity and a profound comprehension of user values, technology becomes a potent ally in the endeavor to improve human life.

CHAPTER 6

Purposeful Practice:
Designing a
Right Livelihood

6.1 Meaningful Experiences: The Essence of UX

The concept of *Right Livelihood* provides a comprehensive viewpoint on the development of user experiences and arises as a guiding beacon at the fascinating intersection of UX design and Buddhist philosophy. This chapter delves into the paradigm-shifting implementation of the *Right Livelihood* principle in the field of user experience design.

The principle has traditionally centered around doing no harm and promoting general well-being. *Right Livelihood* goes beyond the usual design goals in the world of digital experience development, suggesting that we make things that not only work but also improve and enrich people's lives.

> By moving the emphasis from superficial considerations of usability and aesthetics to more substantial interactions between the product and its end users, this theory reimagines user experience design at its core. It is about creating connections that go beyond practicality and into meaningful and pleasurable experiences with technology, through emotional resonance in the design of user interfaces.

By bringing *Right Livelihood* into user experience design, we can take a more comprehensive view of how our decisions will affect both the user and society at large. It is a challenge for designers to think about how their products may affect people in the future, making sure they help people and do not hurt them.

With this method, you need to put yourself in the shoes of the user and try to comprehend their wants and needs from a human rather than a purely functional one. It is about making venues that are welcoming, interesting, and supportive of users' emotional and mental health through digital encounters.

> The term *Right Livelihood* in user experience design takes on a new meaning when applied to the creation of experiences that are good for people and the world at large, bringing together the aims of digital design with those of individual and collective fulfillment.

An additional aspect of Right Livelihood in user experience design is a dedication to sustainable and ethical business practices. As designers, we must consider the effects on the environment of our decisions and work to make our digital products as sustainable as possible.

Additionally, we need to remove obstacles and make sure that all of our designs are accessible so that we can meet the needs of a wide variety of users. Our work will be more in line with the larger good and help create a more ethical and socially responsible digital world if we incorporate these ethical issues into UX design from the start.

Simply put, *Right Livelihood* is a path towards making digital experiences that are incredibly human-centered when applied to UX design. It is a promise to design with empathy, awareness, and a deep regard for the welfare of people and society, in addition to technical knowledge and imagination. Instead of focusing on improving design processes, this chapter aims to redefine UX design's role in creating a future where technology can improve people's lives and the world at large.

Taking this tack will lead to a future where digital en-counters are uplifting for the soul as well as the body and mind, and not only in terms of functionality.

Designing for Positive Impact and Well-being

It is our ultimate aim to design digital experiences that have a beneficial impact on more than just the user journey; we want to make a difference in people's lives and the world at large. At the end of this path, the focus shifts from design's functional or aesthetically pleasing purposes to its ability to generate a holistic, beneficial impact on users and the community at large.

When designing digital experiences, it is important to keep consumers' psychological and emotional well-being in mind alongside practical considerations like ease of use and aesthetic appeal. This method necessitates a consider-ate and sympathetic evaluation of the ways in which our design decisions influence the mental health of users, their interactions with their physical surroundings, and their per-ception and participation in the digital realm.

Digital product designers must walk a fine line between making entertaining and rewarding designs and keeping in mind that their work may have a positive effect on the us-er's emotional and mental health.

For this to work, you need to know your consumers in-side and out, including their mental and emotional makeup. The goal is to create online communities that are welcom-ing to all users, easy to navigate, and conducive to produc-tive dialogue.

By creating an environment where people feel appreciated, understood, and cared for, these spaces may help build a strong digital ecosystem where everyone can thrive.

In addition, this method of user experience design is all about thinking ahead to the bigger picture of how our digital products will affect society and ethics. The goal is to create experiences that are good for people in the here and now, but also for society as a whole in the long run.

> Designing interfaces that discourage negative behaviors like online harassment or disinformation could be part of this, or it could involve features that encourage positive behaviors like collaboration, kindness, and mindfulness. All it takes is a forward-thinking approach to design, the ability to foresee societal demands and problems, and the ability to create digital experiences that can handle and adjust to these changing dynamics.

A dedication to making a positive impact and promoting well-being via the use of our skills and creativity is at the heart of designing for *Right Livelihood* in UX. On this adventure, we will rethink the function of technology in our daily lives and strive to imagine and build digital experiences that do more than just satisfy our basic necessities; they will improve our health, happiness, and the fabric of our communities.

As designers, we have the power to shape a future where technology is more than just a means to an end — it can be a force for good, a means to individual development and the well-being of society as a whole — by adopting this perspective.

Ethical Considerations in Creating UX

We greatly enhance the ethical aspects of our job by including *Right Livelihood* into UX design. This approach encourages designers to thoroughly consider the impact their inventions will have in the future. It is about realizing how design decisions impact user behavior, privacy, and quality of life in general.

Integrating this principle into user experience design goes beyond just following industry standards. It signifies a strong dedication to ethical principles that emphasize openness, safeguarding user data, and a thoughtful approach to designing information and interactions. As part of their ethical obligation, designers should think about the impact their digital goods have on the environment and push for more sustainable practices.

It is the duty of user experience designers, according to this paradigm, to make sure that our products help people in the long run, not just in the short term. It entails thinking about the ethical consequences of decisions ahead of time and analyzing anything from data management techniques to user interface design.

Taking precautions to safeguard user information, treating user data with the highest regard, and creating interesting interactions while being mindful of the user's emotional and mental well-being are all parts of this process.

In addition, keeping to UX design ethics requires us to think about how our work may affect society at large. The key is to be aware of how your designs might affect public opinion, societal mores, and cultural conventions. We take into account the possible social effects of our products and strive to build digital experiences that encourage positive behaviors, inclusivity, and understanding as a result of this awareness, which leads to a more comprehensive approach to design.

Making things that serve their intended purpose while also improving people's lives, strengthening communities, and advancing society as a whole is what we mean when we talk about socially responsible design.

It is an open call to break free from the constraints of conventional design methods and go on a quest to make digital experiences that are socially significant, ethically rich, and technically sound. *Right Livelihood* outlines a set of principles that user experience designers can follow to help create a digital world where technology is a tool for good in the fight for a more just, caring, and environmentally friendly society. *Taking this tactic in design is not just the way the industry is structured; it is a statement about our dedication to making a good impact on people's lives and society as a whole.*

6.2 Buddhist Design Ethics: Socially Responsible Practice

The use of Buddhist ethics in UX design represents a revolutionary change toward a more socially conscious methodology. These deeply ingrained Buddhist ideas provide a rich context for reconsidering and altering design approaches. By adhering to these principles, designers are broadening their scope beyond the user's immediate demands and embracing a deeper commitment to environmental sustainability and societal well-being.

With this change, a new path toward good societal contribution and ethical mindfulness in the production of digital experiences begins one that goes beyond simple usability and user happiness.

Mindfulness in UX design refers to a more acute understanding of the effects of design decisions, encouraging designers to think about the wider implications of their work on people and communities. This increased consciousness promotes a design approach that thoughtfully weighs the long-term effects of products on the lives of consumers and social systems.

When it comes to UX design, compassion means making experiences that are not only intuitive and easy to use but also compassionate and inclusive. It means taking into account the wide diversity of human experiences and making an effort to fairly serve the requirements of each and every user. This kind-hearted approach produces designs that become more than instruments; they become pillars of support in the lives of their users, improving their entire quality of life and augmenting their well-being.

In addition, incorporating ethical responsibility into UX design necessitates addressing moral conundrums and obstacles in a proactive manner. It entails making deliberate choices that are consistent with moral principles and making sure that designs both adhere to and encourage moral behavior from users.

Designers are urged to implement sustainable methods in order to lessen the ecological impact of their digital goods and to foster a more sustainable relationship between technology and the environment. This dedication also extends to environmental considerations. UX designers are fostering experiences that resonate with a deeper sense of purpose and responsibility by incorporating these Buddhist ethical principles, and they are making a positive impact on a world that is more moral, compassionate, and sustainable.

The Pillars of Buddhist Design Ethics

The incorporation of Buddhist design principles offers a profound and multifaceted approach to developing digital experiences in the ever-evolving field of UX design. The fundamental principles of this strategy are ethical responsiveness, compassion, and mindfulness, each of which is vital in creating a design philosophy that is not only practical but also morally and socially conscious.

Mindfulness:

In the world of UX design, the highly ethically grounded practice of mindfulness is invaluable. It represents an elevated consciousness and thoughtfulness that goes well beyond the obvious qualities of utility and aesthetic appeal. Design mindfulness is taking a broad view and carefully assessing how design choices will affect the world more broadly and thoroughly.

It entails a careful and introspective process in which every facet of the design, from the tiniest interface component to the complete user journey, is carefully considered for any potential long-term repercussions on users and society as a whole.

To integrate mindfulness into UX design, one must adopt a future-oriented perspective. Designers are urged to consider how their creations might affect user behavior and society standards in the long run, looking beyond the ease and instant gratification of their goods.

> This involves taking into account problems like user dependency, where the accessibility and user-friendliness of digital interfaces may encourage excessive or addictive use. Being mindful also entails being aware of the dangers of information overload, in which users may become confused or overwhelmed by the wealth of available information. It also entails being aware of the potential for abuse and making sure that designs do not unintentionally encourage bad behaviors or damaging relationships.

This thoughtful approach to UX design is an active, continuous dedication to moral and responsible creation rather than a passive process. It involves continuously challenging and reevaluating our design decisions to make sure they support an all-encompassing vision of user welfare and societal benefit.

When it comes to design, mindfulness cultivates an atmosphere where creativity and responsibility coexist with innovation. Through the integration of this idea into the design process, designers may create digital experiences that enhance consumers' overall quality of life while simultaneously satisfying their current demands.

Essentially, mindfulness in UX design is a paradigm-shifting technique that changes the way designers approach their work. It is a dedication to producing digital products that serve as catalysts for constructive change and individual development rather than just convenient tools.

By taking this careful approach, we can make sure that the digital experiences we design today are not only cutting-edge and beautiful to look at but also ethically sound, nurturing, and long-term beneficial for both users and society.

By adopting mindfulness, UX designers demonstrate a profound and careful knowledge of the complex link between our products and the world they inhabit, and they take a major step towards a future where technology improves human lives in a comprehensive and sustainable manner.

Compassion:
One of the main principles of Buddhism is compassion, and this is evident in the field of UX design. In this situation, compassion shows up as a deep sense of empathy and dedication to comprehending and meeting the needs and experiences of the user.

This method of approaching design aims to produce inclusive, approachable, highly sensitive, and deeply empathic experiences. It is a design ethos that takes into account the variety of human experiences and values them, accommodating users with varying capacities, backgrounds, and circumstances.

> Compassionate design is about truly engaging with users, knowing their individual challenges and desires, and expressing this understanding in every area of the design. It goes well beyond technical accessibility.

Creating digital experiences with consideration for the emotional and psychological effects they have on users is the first step in integrating compassion into UX design. This goes beyond simply building user-friendly interfaces; it also entails developing encounters that are supportive and emotionally enlightening.

It is acknowledging that people approach digital products from a variety of emotional and life experiences, and designing with empathy, comfort, and understanding in mind. In order to make sure that consumers feel appreciated, respected, and cared for from the very first point of contact to the very last, compassionate design considers the whole user journey. It involves creating digital environments that support and nurture users, enhance their emotional well-being, and are not just productive and efficient.

Furthermore, a strong commitment to diversity is necessary for compassionate UX design. It entails making a concerted effort to comprehend and account for the entire range of human variability, including individuals who are frequently left out of the design process.

This entails taking into account consumers with various socioeconomic origins, cultural backgrounds, and physical and cognitive capacities. In order to ensure that digital products are not just usable by a diverse variety of consumers but also personally meaningful to them, compassionate design pushes for universal access to technology. It is about dismantling boundaries in the digital sphere and producing experiences that are as varied and complex as the users.

> Compassion in UX design is essentially about encouraging a deeper relationship than just surface-level interaction between the user and the digital product. It is a comprehensive strategy that sees technology as a way to improve human connection and experience rather than only as a tool.

UX designers use a more compassionate and humane approach to technology by incorporating compassion into the design process, producing digital experiences that are not only helpful and functional but also emotionally satisfying and supportive. This strategy not only improves customer happiness but also helps create a digital environment that is more welcoming, compassionate, and understanding.

Ethical Responsiveness:
A crucial paradigm that emphasizes being proactive and watchful when it comes to the ethical ramifications of digital technologies is ethical responsiveness. This idea goes beyond accepted design conventions and explores the

more profound role that designers have in influencing the moral implications of technology. In UX design, ethical responsiveness refers to proactively recognizing and resolving the many ethical issues that could come up throughout the design phase. This duty covers a wide range of topics, such as protecting user privacy, closing the digital divide, and taking the environment into account when making design choices.

> A higher degree of awareness and planning is necessary for ethical responsiveness, as it calls for designers to anticipate and negotiate difficult ethical situations. It entails an ongoing process of analyzing and reanalyzing design decisions to make sure they adhere to strict ethical guidelines.

In the context of data privacy, for example, ethical responsiveness entails not just following the law but also taking proactive measures to safeguard user data in order to maintain user confidence. In a similar vein, in order to overcome the digital divide, designs must be inclusive and accessible in order to reach underprivileged and marginalized communities and advance digital equity.

Environmental considerations are also a part of ethical responsiveness in UX design. In this day and age, designers have an increasingly important responsibility to consider the environment while making decisions. This could be using eco-friendly materials, making the most use of available resources, or designing for durability as opposed to obsolescence. It is about being aware of the ecological footprint that digital items leave behind and making an effort to reduce such effects. Therefore, ethical responsiveness takes into account the wider effects of design on the environment in addition to the immediate user experience.

To sum up, ethical responsiveness is a crucial element of modern UX design, incorporating ethical issues into the process without any problems. It is a call to action for designers to be morally watchful, making sure that their works follow the values of moral integrity in addition to meeting practical and aesthetic requirements.

UX designers have a critical role to play in creating a digital environment that is not only effective and entertaining but also ethical, just, and sustainable by adopting ethical responsiveness. This method elevates the field of UX design and establishes it as a vital player in the moral advancement of technology in society.

Sustainability:
Sustainability is a fundamental commitment to environmental stewardship in the digital sphere and is a crucial extension of ethical responsiveness in UX design.

Sustainability is a basic value that directs the entire design process in the framework of Buddhist design ethics, not just something to take into account. This dedication pushes UX designers to thoughtfully consider the environmental effects of their digital goods and encourages them to make ethical decisions that drastically lessen the impact on the environment.

With this approach to sustainable design, every detail must be carefully considered, from the choice of resources and materials for digital interfaces to the final disposal or recycling of digital products, as well as their whole lifecycle. It involves promoting a design philosophy that places ecological balance and the long-term health of the ecosystem first.

Sustainable UX design considers all options and considers how each one might affect the environment. It is recommended that designers look into more environmentally friendly options for their designs, whether they are used in hardware components or digital infrastructure.

This could be lowering digital clutter, promoting the use of renewable energy sources in data centers, or enhancing software for energy efficiency. Furthermore, the idea of designing with lifespan and durability is a bigger component of sustainable UX design. *By supporting designs that persist and remain relevant over time, this strategy counteracts the prevalent culture of obsolescence in technology, minimizes the need for frequent replacements, and reduces electronic waste.*

Furthermore, the field of sustainable UX design encompasses user interaction and behavior. The challenge for designers is to create digital experiences that quietly support and promote sustainable practices while simultaneously engaging consumers.

This can entail adding elements that promote environmental awareness or creating user interfaces that reward eco-friendly actions. Thus, sustainable UX design influences real-world behaviors and adds to a wider sustainability culture, reaching beyond the confines of the digital screen.

In summary, the focus on sustainability in UX design, in line with Buddhist design principles, represents a significant turn in the direction of a more ecologically aware methodology in the industry. It is a comprehensive viewpoint that sees digital products as essential parts of a greater ecological system rather than as separate things.

UX designers can significantly reduce the environmental impact of technology by implementing sustainable design techniques. This will pave the road for a time when ecological sustainability and digital innovation coexist together.

> With this approach, we can be confident that the digital experiences of today are not only made with environmental care but also that future generations will feel responsible for the digital advancements we make now and that they will not undermine the integrity of the environment in the future.

The four pillars of Buddhist design ethics — compassion, sustainability, ethical responsiveness, and mindfulness — provide a comprehensive and multidimensional framework for UX design. This methodology guarantees that digital products are socially and ethically responsible in addition to improving their usefulness and aesthetics.

Through the use of these principles, UX designers may produce digital experiences that are cutting-edge in terms of technology but also in line with the greater goals of societal progress and human welfare.

Fostering Social Responsibility Through Design

The adoption of Buddhist design ethics signals a dramatic change in the direction of fostering a pervasive social responsibility culture within the design community. This ethical paradigm directs designers toward the creation of digital experiences that are not just effective and visually appealing but also socially and morally based and go beyond the traditional goals of usefulness and aesthetic appeal.

By adhering to these principles, UX designers go beyond simply developing digital interfaces and instead become engaged participants in improving society by applying their knowledge to address and ameliorate more general social problems. This design methodology entails a dedicated endeavor to promote digital literacy, increase digital accessibility for underrepresented populations, and advocate for ecologically friendly practices.

Emphasizing digital accessibility is a crucial component of using design to promote social responsibility. This entails creating products that are both widely accessible and specifically designed to cater to the requirements of groups that might not otherwise be able to access digital technology, such as people with disabilities or those from disadvantaged backgrounds.

UX designers may contribute to closing the digital divide and guaranteeing that all societal segments can reap the benefits of technology by emphasizing accessibility. This dedication also includes promoting and putting into practice inclusive and sympathetic design solutions, which will help create a more just and equitable digital environment.

Another essential component of using UX design to promote social responsibility is the promotion of digital literacy. Equipping people with the know-how to efficiently navigate and use technology is essential in an increasingly digital environment.

The work of designers is crucial in this attempt as they create interfaces that are easy to use and encourage digital involvement, especially for individuals who may not be as tech-savvy. UX designers may contribute to the demystification of technology by making it more understandable and accessible to a larger audience. This will increase the digital literacy of society.

In addition, promoting sustainable design methods is a crucial part of UX design's social duty. It is becoming more and more important for designers to take the ecological impact of their work into account as environmental consciousness rises.

This entails making deliberate decisions to minimize damage to the environment, like using sustainable materials, cutting down on electrical waste, and increasing energy efficiency. UX designers can help create digital goods that are not just creative and useful, but also ecologically conscious by including these factors into the design process. This will pave the way for a more sustainable future.

Fostering social responsibility through design is essentially about using UX to positively influence society. It is about realizing how our work affects society at large and making an effort to design digital experiences that benefit society as a whole as well as specific users.

UX designers may make a significant contribution to creating a more just, inclusive, and sustainable digital world by adopting Buddhist design ethics. They can use their creativity and skill to close societal divides and promote a more morally and socially conscious society.

Sustainable and Ethical Design Solutions

The application of Buddhist design ethics to UX design places a fresh emphasis on ethical integrity and sustainability. By using this strategy, designers become more than just designers of digital things; they become custodians of a sustainable and socially conscious future.

This ethical framework's core value is a dedication to reducing the environmental impact of digital products. It is recommended that designers embrace a green mindset, looking for creative methods to lower carbon footprints and improve sustainability.

This environmentally responsible approach to design entails making deliberate decisions in all areas, from choosing eco-friendly materials for physical components to optimizing resource utilization in digital activities. Reducing the ecological impact of our digital footprint is the aim of creating technologically sophisticated but ecologically conscious digital experiences.

A move toward long-term design is another aspect of sustainability in UX design. This idea goes against the fast obsolescence ethos that permeates the tech sector. It is the goal of designers to produce digital goods that are both functionally and historically relevant for a long time.

This methodology not only mitigates electronic waste but also cultivates a more enduring link between technology and its users. Designers may contribute to a more sustainable digital ecosystem by reducing the cycle of constant consumption and waste through the creation of products that are robust and flexible.

Ethical design solutions in UX are firmly rooted in the values of openness, truthfulness, and integrity, in addition to sustainability. This ethical component guarantees that the design process and the final goods meet the most stringent moral requirements.

It entails having open lines of contact with consumers to make sure they are well-informed and have faith in the goods they use. In addition to putting user privacy and data security first, ethical design upholds users' rights and dignity throughout the digital experience. UX designers may produce digital products that are not just trustworthy and considerate of user autonomy, but also highly effective by including these ethical considerations into the design process.

Supporting sustainable and ethical design in user experience (UX) goes beyond professional guidelines to serve as a call to action for designers to adopt a more responsible and conscientious approach to their work. By incorporating Buddhist ethics into their work, designers play a vital role in creating a digital environment that strikes a balance between effectiveness and user-friendliness and compassion, morality, and social responsibility.

This chapter emphasizes the value of ethical mindfulness in design and calls on designers to think about how their work may affect people more broadly as well as society and the environment.

To sum up, ethical and sustainable design solutions in user experience mark a revolutionary change in our understanding of technology and design. UX designers are in a unique position to develop digital experiences that satisfy user demands while also promoting a more ethical, socially conscious, and sustainable digital world when they adopt the design ethics of Buddhism.

By bringing UX design into line with the larger objectives of ethical integrity, environmental stewardship, and societal well-being, this method enhances the field. It is a path toward utilizing technology as a potent force for good change and human enrichment in an increasingly digital society, rather than just as a tool for efficiency and convenience.

Designing
with Diligence

NAVIGATING THE EFFORTFUL TERRAIN

By following the deep teachings of Buddhism in the field of UX design, *Section IV: Designing with Diligence* encapsulates the path to mastery and greatness. This part goes into detail about the complicated and often hard road of commitment, constant improvement, and careful attention to detail in the design process. In Buddhist thought, diligence is more than just working hard over and over again. It means doing your work with awareness and purpose, showing traits like care, thoroughness, and a never-ending drive for greatness.

This is the beginning of a series of articles that will talk about different parts of diligence in UX design. To become a UX designer, you need to know that your career will always be one of learning and growing.

Digital design is always evolving because new technologies, user wants, and social changes happen all the time. To get around this area, you have to consistently stay aware, flexible, and proactive. To do this, you have to keep learning new skills, researching users, and keeping up with the latest tech trends and social issues.

When it comes to the hard work of UX design, care also means paying close attention to every detail. A lot of thought and care went into every pixel, interaction, and user flow, showing great respect for the experience of the user. This careful approach is not just about being good at technology; it is also about making digital experiences that are not only useful but also highly satisfying and emotional.

Being careful in design means finding the right balance between being creative and being useful, between being innovative and being easy to use, and making sure that every part works together to make the experience seamless and enjoyable for the user.

When you create with diligence, you also make an effort to balance speed and quality. Keeping a high level of quality can be hard in a field where production is often fast, and deadlines are short. In this case, diligence means finding that balance and making sure that the rush to meet goals does not hurt the design's integrity and quality. It means setting up routines and procedures that make things run more smoothly without losing care for details or the needs of users.

There is also an ethical aspect to carefully handling the difficult terrain of UX design. It means being responsible and careful in every part of the design, from protecting user privacy and data to making sure everyone can use and access the design. Being diligent in this case means sticking to moral standards and making sure that the digital products we make are not only new and easy to use, but also good for society and morale.

Finally, the beginning of *Designing with Diligence* sets the tone for a part that really gets to the heart of what it means to be a diligent UX designer. It is an invitation to start a path of careful craftsmanship, lifelong learning, and moral awareness. We are excited about the challenges and chances that come with aiming for excellence in UX design. We want to make digital experiences that are not only useful and fun, but also morally sound and deeply beneficial for users and society as a whole.

CHAPTER 7

Iterative Excellence: Nurturing Right Effort

7.1 User-Centricity in Focus: Right Effort in UX

The idea of *Right Effort*, which has its origins in Buddhist philosophy, has become an important principle in user experience design. *Right Effort* is a key concept in the quest for design excellence, and this chapter delves into its deep relevance to creating digital experiences with the user in mind. *Right Effort* in user experience design means paying close attention to detail and making deliberate decisions in order to create something that not only meets but also exceeds the actual requirements and expectations of the target audience.

Because of the dynamic nature of this approach, a methodology that can adapt quickly to changing user needs and technological developments is essential. Assuring that every design decision is deliberate and implemented with purpose, *Right Effort* in user experience is defined by a harmonious blend of accuracy, imagination, and empathy.

> *Right Effort* in user experience design, delving further, refers to establishing a basic rapport with the user and learning about their needs. It is about committing to lifelong learning — about users, their habits, the obstacles they face, and the goals they want to achieve.

For this, you will need to devote a lot of time and energy to study, communicate with users sympathetically, and examine user data and comments thoroughly. We aim to foster a design approach that is sensitive to user experiences and informed by their insights. *Right Effort* is based on this cycle of learning and applying, where designers continuously adjust and improve their work to meet user goals, guaranteeing that the final result is meaningful and applicable in addition to being functional.

Further, the *Right Effort* principle in user experience design represents the ever-changing character of the design procedure. It acknowledges that there is no end to the never-ending quest to create exceptional digital experiences. The path is characterized by a continuous loop of brainstorming, making, testing, and improving.

> *Right Effort* designers are not content with settling for a single solution; instead, they are enthusiastic about trying new things, testing their designs thoroughly, and being receptive to criticism and suggestions. In addition to improving the design's efficacy and quality, this method makes sure it can handle changes in human needs and technology without breaking down.

A well-rounded and balanced approach to digital experience creation is what *Right Effort* in UX design speaks to. A true commitment to excellence goes beyond technical skill; it includes a strong understanding of users' needs and an unwavering determination to meet those demands as they change over time. The concepts of *Right Effort* guide designers toward deliberate and intentional creation; the result is digital experiences that serve their intended purpose while also touching people on a profound emotional level and improving their relationship with technology.

Understanding and Empathizing with Users

Consistently putting yourself in the shoes of the user is key to the *Right Effort* notion of user experience design. This dedication goes beyond simple analytics and data collection, touching on a deeper investigation of the consumers' actual motivations and influences. Understanding the complete range of a user's experience requires delving into the complex web of their feelings, actions, and underlying motives.

An extensive user research procedure, including techniques like in-depth interviews, detailed surveys, and exhaustive usability testing, is necessary for this strategy. Gathering quantitative data is important, but adding qualitative insights can help paint a more complete picture of the user's experience.

> As part of their quest for compassionate design, user experience professionals investigate the backstories and environments that influence how people engage with digital goods. Understanding people's hidden expectations and latent wishes is equally as important as listening to their apparent needs and wants. By imagining the product through the eyes of the user and going through the emotional roller coaster that is the user experience, designers may better empathize with their customers and create more meaningful products. When designers put themselves in the customer's purview, they create designs that are more than just practical; they strike an emotional chord with their target audience.

On top of that, user experience design is all about learning and growing with the people. It acknowledges that user wants and preferences are dynamic, meaning they alter and adapt over time in response to factors such as new technologies, shifting cultural norms, and personal experiences.

Hence, designers must consistently revisit and reevaluate their comprehension of the user base, as user research and empathy are ongoing processes. This unwavering dedication to comprehending users guarantees that design choices stay pertinent and adaptable to the constantly evolving user environment.

It is all about digging deep into the user's emotional and psychological characteristics, rather than only looking at the surface levels of user engagement. User experience designers can make products that are more than just functional — they can make goods that connect with people emotionally by basing design decisions on this thorough understanding and empathy. This method does more than improve usability; it establishes a long-lasting bond between the product and its user based on mutual understanding, empathy, and trust.

Iterative Design and Continuous Improvement

The *Right Effort* idea in UX design is a manifestation of the iterative design philosophy and the unwavering quest for ongoing enhancement. This way of thinking acknowledges that the path of design is a never-ending one, characterized by continuous advancement and adaptation rather than a fixed destination.

This iterative design process views the process of creating digital experiences as a continuous loop that involves invention and refining. When designers take this approach, they become fully involved in a process where ideas and designs are just the start. Every iteration entails building prototypes, putting them into practice, getting user input, and then going back to the drawing board to improve and polish. The knowledge that human requirements and technical environments are dynamic and always evolving drives this never-ending loop.

Iterative processes are essential in the field of user experience to keep up with the constantly changing needs and preferences of users. Users' comments and actions while interacting with digital products offer priceless data that guide future design advancements. The ongoing feedback and modification process makes sure that the UX design stays current, practical, and user-focused.

It makes it possible for designers to react quickly to changes in market trends, consumer expectations, or technology breakthroughs. This process' iterative nature also makes it easier to comprehend the user experience, giving designers the ability to fine-tune and optimize each component of the product for both usability and maximum effect.

Furthermore, within the UX community, the iterative design process promotes an environment of experimentation and learning. It inspires designers to embrace risk-taking, investigate novel concepts, and embrace experimentation. This kind of thinking is essential for innovation and development because it enables designers to push the envelope of what is feasible and find fresh approaches to issues.

Iterative design also fosters resilience and adaptation by teaching designers to see errors as opportunities for useful learning rather than as setbacks. Every iteration serves as a teaching tool for what works and what doesn't, assisting designers in developing more sophisticated and potent solutions.

Iterative design and continual improvement are the ways that *Right Effort* in UX is essentially about accepting the fluid and changing nature of design. It is a pledge to never give up and to constantly look for new, improved, and creative solutions. This method seeks to stay ahead of the curve by consistently pushing the boundaries and improving the user experience, rather than just keeping up with the rapidly evolving landscape of technology and user needs.

UX designers exhibit a proactive, sensitive, and forward-thinking perspective by taking an iterative and continuous approach to improvement, which guarantees that their work stays at the forefront of innovation and user happiness.

Ethical Considerations and User Advocacy

The incorporation of *Right Effort* into user experience design showcases a strong dedication to ethical considerations and unwavering support for the user. Here, the needs and welfare of users are considered essential, and UX design moves beyond the purely pragmatic pursuit of corporate goals. Here, user experience designers take on the role of user advocates, fighting for the rights, preferences, and needs of users in all their designs.

> Among the many goals of this advocacy is the guarantee of user privacy, the expansion of digital product accessibility, and the general improvement of user engagement and happiness.

Aiming to strike a balance between commercial objectives and the ethical consequences of design decisions is essential to upholding ethical considerations in user experience design. This position requires designers to walk a fine line between serving business interests and advocating for users, with the latter often requiring them to take the lead.

This necessitates making important design decisions while keeping the user experience in mind. Asking questions like "Is this design accessible to all users?" and "Does this product improve the user's life without taking advantage of their vulnerabilities?" are all part of this process. By asking these kinds of questions, we can make sure that the design process is about more than simply making things that look good and work well; it is also about making things that are ethical and that help people.

In addition, the concept of *Right Effort* in user experience design refers to the dedication to making digital experiences accessible and inclusive. To achieve this goal, we must ensure that our products are accessible to people of diverse abilities, socioeconomic statuses, and life experiences.

It entails actively striving to avoid digital products that marginalize or exclude any group and having a thorough comprehension of the wide range of user experiences. When we talk about inclusive design, we are not just talking about meeting accessibility requirements; we are talking about really putting the needs of all users first.

Ultimately, when it comes to user experience design, *Right Effort* represents a comprehensive strategy that prioritizes honesty and standing up for users. Designing with a conscience means considering the users' needs and happiness alongside financial considerations. Adopting this stance, user experience designers fight for an ethically sound, inclusive, and compassionate digital society that is also profitable and efficient.

By prioritizing ethical concerns and user advocacy, we guarantee that our products will make a beneficial impact on the digital world. The products will improve users' lives and help create a more fair and considerate online community.

Collaboration and Team Dynamics

When it comes to user experience design, the *Right Effort* idea has a significant impact on both the design process and team dynamics. With this idea in mind, it is crucial to build a team whose members — designers, developers, stakeholders, and everyone else — are all pulling in the same direction.

Crucial in such a setting are open lines of communication, mutual regard, and a dedication to the user's needs. Technically solid, user-centric, and innovative products are the result of a culture that values and leverages the unique expertise and perspective of each team member.

The foundation of any successful UX team is effective communication. People are able to share ideas, overcome obstacles, and find solutions when they communicate in a way that is clear, open, and kind. *Right Effort* provides a framework for the workplace where communication goes beyond simply relaying information; it also aims to cultivate empathy and understanding among team members.

Engaging in active listening allows for the thoughtful consideration of each member's perspectives, while also facilitating the exchange of constructive comments. In this kind of collaborative setting, people are more likely to share their thoughts and feelings, which in turn leads to better, more user-centered design.

Essential to the *Right Effort* principle in team dynamics is a collective dedication to the needs of the end user. By maintaining a singular emphasis, we can guarantee that the user's wants and needs are considered at every stage of the design process, from the most basic aspects to more high-level strategic decisions.

It is about making sure that everyone in the team, no matter their position, sees things from the user's point of view and works to connect the team's goals with improving the user experience. With a shared focus on the needs of the end user, the team is able to design products that go above and beyond what users expect, providing them with rewarding and life-improving experiences.

Innovation and problem-solving are team activities in teams where the *Right Effort* mentality permeates. In this team setting, everyone is free to share their thoughts and opinions, which encourages innovation and exploration. Instead of solving problems in isolation, this team-based method of innovation makes sure that different perspectives and ideas are included at every stage.

By tapping on everyone's knowledge and imagination, the team is better able to take on difficult problems. Team satisfaction and cohesiveness are both boosted by this dynamic, which in turn leads to better design solutions.

The *Right Effort* principle in user experience design, to sum up, has far-reaching implications for group dynamics and cooperation. User experience teams who adhere to this principle create a culture that values open dialogue, mutual regard, putting the user first, and working together to solve problems.

This chapter emphasizes the significance of fostering a culture of collaboration in user experience design. In this setting, everyone works together to create digital experiences that are great in functionality but also considerate and focused on the user.

When applied here, the term *Right Effort* refers to the process of assembling groups of people who are committed to improving the digital environment and the user experience in a way that is both efficient and productive. In order to create a digital world that is more inclusive, ethical, and user-centric, this journey asks teams to

> collaborate carefully, intelligently, and compassionately, utilizing their combined abilities and insights.

7.2 Diligence in Design: A Buddhist Perspective

The incorporation of Buddhist-inspired thoroughness into user experience design provides a deep and comprehensive framework for making digital products. Here we explore how the idea of diligence, which has its origins in Buddhist philosophy, influences the creative procedure.

To be diligent in user experience design is to approach the task of creating user experiences with care and attention, rather than just being persistent. Careful attention to every detail of the design is required throughout this procedure. This method guarantees that designs are in harmony with user needs and are both visually beautiful and ethically sound.

Mindful Attention to Detail

A meticulous UX designer is characterized by their intense attention to detail in designing the user interface. The method digs deep into the little details that can take a product's interaction with the user from ordinary to extraordinary, going above and beyond surface-level design considerations.

> Designers must pay close attention to detail by analyzing each component for its technical and aesthetic value as well as its function in the bigger picture of the user journey. A thorough examination of how each component — icon, layout, interaction, and button — works together to provide a unified and natural experience for the user is part of this approach.

Paying close attention to detail strikes a balance between being aesthetically refined and knowing the user's needs with empathy. It is the responsibility of diligent designers to build user interfaces that are aesthetically pleasing and intuitively tailored to the needs and habits of the target audience.

This calls for an intricate understanding of how aesthetics affects usability and user involvement in the design process. To be a good designer, you need to know how your decisions will make people feel and think, not just how they will look. To anticipate the wants, preferences, and possible difficulties that users may face when interacting with the product, this degree of empathy in design is essential.

Thinking Forward to User Reactions and Needs

An important part of user experience design is being able to foresee and meet users' requirements. Data analysis, feedback loops, and user testing are just a few of the methods that conscientious designers utilize to learn about user behavior.

Designers obtain useful insights that direct the improvement process by carefully watching how users engage with various interface components. Upholding a meticulous degree of design relies on this continuous cycle of observation, learning, and modification. This procedure guarantees that the product can deliver a compelling and enjoyable user experience in addition to its functionality and usefulness.

Final Reflections on Design Detail

Finally, a strong dedication to the user is the bedrock of careful UX design, which in turn requires careful attention to detail. It is a method that requires you to think about every part of the design and make sure it helps the user. Professionals in user experience design make items that connect with consumers on a profound level by adopting this meticulous and compassionate approach to design.

Digital experiences that stand out are those that pay close attention to every little detail, allowing them to become more than just tools for users—they become extensions of their relationships, preferences, and lifestyles. By being meticulous, UX designers are able to shape digital experiences that are genuinely focused on the user, easy to use, and beneficial.

Continuous Learning and Adaptation

Keeping up with changing consumer preferences, developing design trends, and expanding technologies is not just necessary for designers who strive for excellence; it is their passion. Astute UX designers are aware that official training and project completion are only the beginning of their educational path.

Rather, it is a lifetime dedication to personal improvement. This dedication to lifelong learning is actively searching out new information, whether via specialized training programs, industry conferences, interaction with UX professionals, or keeping up with the most recent findings and writings. It is a way of thinking that prioritizes inquisitiveness and an insatiable desire to learn, understanding that the UX industry is a dynamic and ever-evolving profession.

> Adaptability is a prime example of diligence in UX design, which goes beyond knowledge gathering. Adjusting and pivoting designs is crucial in an industry where technology capabilities and consumer needs are always changing. A diligent designer is not inflexible in their methods; rather, they are adaptable and receptive to fresh data and criticism.

This flexibility entails seeing each test result, measurement, and user comment as a chance for improvement. It entails being willing to review and rethink products when new information becomes available in order to maintain the final product's relevance, efficacy, and alignment with customer needs. People view this ongoing process of adaptation as an exciting chance to create and succeed rather than as a challenge.

The foundation of conscientious UX design is the interaction between ongoing learning and adaptability. Learning influences adaptability, which, in turn, encourages more learning. Devoted designers are better able to make well-informed design selections as they immerse themselves in the most recent market knowledge.

At the same time, no textbook can match the practical insights they have gained from their experiences in modifying designs in response to feedback from the actual world. As a result of this cycle, designers are continually developing, maturing, and honing their craft — a self-reinforcing cycle. It results in a thorough comprehension of the "why" as well as the "how" behind UX design decisions, enabling a deeper engagement with the task at hand and a more significant influence on the user.

This method aims to embrace a mindset of constant growth and responsiveness rather than just teaching skills. By following this course, designers make sure that their work stays at the forefront of UX innovation, connecting with consumers and satisfying their constantly changing needs. Such a commitment to learning and flexibility is what sets exceptional designers apart in a sector as dynamic as user experience.

The dedicated UX designer is defined by their unwavering quest for information and their adaptability in putting it to use. This, in turn, influences the future of user experiences.

Ethical and Compassionate Design

This strategy goes beyond just a product's ability to perform and touches on morality and integrity. In this situation, conscientious designers understand full well the wider effects of their choices on society at large as well as on specific consumers.

Since they are aware that every decision made during the design process can have a significant impact, they approach their work with a strong sense of ethical commitment. This commitment entails making certain that their designs respect user privacy, adhere to fairness standards, and refrain from taking advantage of user vulnerabilities. It involves developing goods that serve as users' protectors of their rights and welfare in addition to being useful tools.

A fundamental component of UX diligence is compassionate design, which is based on empathy and comprehension of the user. This aspect of design necessitates a deep understanding of the range of user experiences and backgrounds.

> In order to meet the demands of a diverse variety of consumers, including those with disabilities and those from different cultural and socioeconomic backgrounds, conscientious designers strive to build products that are inclusive and accessible. Creating experiences that are not just simple to use but also understanding and supportive is the goal of compassionate design, which goes beyond standard usability.

By fostering a sense of respect and belonging among users, this strategy turns technology into a positive factor in their lives.

Diligent UX design also entails a proactive approach to ethical responsiveness and user advocacy, in keeping with the precepts of Buddhism. In this sense, designers are active advocates for the user rather than merely passive makers. This advocacy entails continuously considering the effects that design decisions have on people and making changes that put user welfare first.

It involves promoting moral principles throughout design talks and decision-making to make sure that business goals do not take precedence over user needs. Being ethically responsive in UX design also entails keeping up with newly emerging ethical problems, such as those brought on by new technology, and creating solutions that anticipate and deal with them.

This approach to design aims to embody a philosophy of caring, empathy, and responsibility rather than just following ethical norms. Diligent UX designers help to create a digital landscape that is not just efficient and practical but also morally sound and compassionate by including these ethical dimensions in their work.

It is a dedication to developing not only for the here and now, but also for a day when technology complies with the strictest moral guidelines and empathetically meets the wide range of societal demands.

Collaborative Excellence and Team Synergy

In UX design, diligence goes beyond individual work to include team dynamics and collaboration. This design feature highlights how crucial it is for teams to work synergistically, directing their combined efforts toward the realization of a single, cohesive goal.

When a group of people operates as a cohesive unit, achieving common objectives, they each bring special talents and viewpoints to the table, embodying the diligence that stems from Buddhist ideals. This strategy creates an environment at work where cooperation and support among coworkers are not just ideas but also everyday practices. In this setting, team members serve as mentors, collaborators, and colleagues in addition to being teammates, with each one contributing to the development of a culture of excellence among the whole.

Effective communication and mutual respect are essential practices for attentive UX teams to follow in order to achieve synergy. These teams function best when there is a free and honest exchange of ideas, constructive criticism, and respect for other points of view.

By using a communication strategy, the team makes sure that everyone is aware of the consequences of actions and that everyone is on the same page. Respect for one another is equally important since it creates a productive workplace where every team member feels acknowledged and appreciated. Respect in this context goes beyond recognizing one another's abilities and accomplishments to include appreciating each person's viewpoint, experiences, and opinions.

A committed UX team also shares the same goal of excellence and user-centric design. A similar objective unites teams that excel in meticulous design: to produce products that not only meet but also surpass user expectations. The team stays focused and in alignment because of this one vision.

It entails a group effort to design user experiences that are profoundly empathic and user-focused in addition to being practical and aesthetically beautiful. The design process is deeply rooted in a user-centric strategy that ensures the final product accurately reflects the needs and preferences of the users, from preliminary research to final execution.

When it comes to overcoming obstacles and promoting creativity, cooperative UX teams view each other as essential. These teams understand that when different ideas and viewpoints come together during collaborative problem-solving, the best solutions frequently result.

It is the understanding that their combined creativity can result in breakthroughs that might not be achievable separately that motivates team members to experiment, think outside the box, and explore new ideas. In addition to producing more creative and practical design solutions, this collaborative mindset fortifies the group and fosters a sense of accomplishment and camaraderie.

It captures an all-encompassing method of UX design in which individual abilities and efforts are not as important as teamwork and collaboration. UX teams may produce digital experiences that connect with users more deeply if they adopt rigor in their work.

This chapter highlights the value of a thorough, thoughtful approach to UX design and emphasizes how productive collaboration may result in the development of digital goods that are not just more technically advanced but also morally and emotionally healthy for users. It is evidence of the effectiveness of excellent collaborative work in creating a digital environment that is considerate, welcoming, and enriching for all parties.

CHAPTER 8

Mindful Design: Creating with Right Mindfulness

8.1 Empathetic Design: The Mindfulness in UX

Right Mindfulness, a central tenet of Buddhist philosophy, adds a profoundly transforming dimension to user experience design when applied to this field. This chapter explores the ways in which UX design can incorporate the notion of mindfulness, moving the emphasis from just efficient and attractive to genuinely empathic and user-centric experiences.

Designers practicing mindful design must always have a heightened level of awareness, considering the user's needs and wants in light of each decision. It is all-encompassing because it combines specificity with a broad understanding of the user's context, requirements, and feelings. This thoughtful approach considers more than just the product's appearance and features; it also considers the larger context of the product's impact on the user's life.

An in-depth familiarity with the user is the bedrock of thoughtful UX design. This comprehension goes beyond simple preferences or actions and encompasses a thorough grasp of the user's emotional journey and surroundings:

- It is making an honest attempt to put yourself in the shoes of the user, to understand the problems they encounter and the feelings they go through as a result of using the product.
- By incorporating empathy into design, we can craft user experiences that speak to people on a deeper, more meaningful level.
- The focus should be on the user, who should feel supported, eased, and satisfied by every aspect of the interface and interaction.

From brainstorming to prototyping to final implementation, mindfulness is an integral part of user experience design. Being present while doing user research, brainstorming, prototyping, and testing is essential. Being aware in user research is being open and attentive when gaining insights, paying close attention to the details of user feedback.

Mindfulness during the brainstorming and prototype phases guarantees that design concepts are both novel and in line with user requirements. Mindfulness during testing helps to notice not only how the product works, but also how people feel about it, which allows for a more personalized design based on user feedback.

It is all about making digital things that are useful and beautiful, but also meaningful and bettering people's lives. Practitioners of user experience design who embrace mindfulness adhere to a process of deliberate, user-centered development.

In order to create digital experiences that resonate with consumers and improve their usability and overall technology experience, this chapter stresses the need for mindfulness. It is a way to make the digital world more considerate, empathetic, and user-centered while simultaneously improving the user experience.

The Role of Empathy in Mindful UX

At its core, mindful UX design is based on empathy, which influences the whole product development process. An intuitive grasp of the users' experiences, problems, and goals is at the heart of this compassionate approach to design, which goes beyond simple analysis of user data and behavior.

To design with empathy in user experience means to put oneself in the users' shoes, to perceive the world through their eyes, and to experience emotions similar to theirs. To build digital experiences that connect with consumers on a deeper, more emotional level, this level of knowledge is essential.

Recognizing the user's journey in all its complexity and richness means taking into account not only their immediate requirements but also their more profound emotional and psychological states.

The goal of user experience design that prioritizes empathy is to help create products that take users on an emotional journey. This trip is just as significant as the actual experience of visiting a website or app.

> By incorporating empathy into their work, UX designers aim to make products that users can relate to on an emotional level while also being easy to use and understand. For this, you need to put yourself in the shoes of a user and try to guess how they could feel when using your product.

To illustrate, when designing with mindfulness and empathy, one considers the potential emotions elicited by a user interface and modifies its components appropriately. The objective is to design goods that do more than just meet needs; they should make the user feel good, which will lead to a stronger bond between the two.

With empathic UX design, the user's emotional requirements are considered at every stage of the product's creation. In addition to being aesthetically beautiful, the interfaces should exude a sense of calm and security.

Instead of interacting with a machine, it should feel more like a chat with a considerate friend. When selecting design elements, we keep in mind how well they communicate empathy and understanding in addition to their aesthetic value.

For instance, we make sure that the language, graphics, and color scheme we utilize fit in with the overall mood and setting of the user's experience. To create a product that is not just used, but also felt and experienced on a deeper level, empathic UX design goes beyond the usual limitations of user interaction.

Mindfulness in User Research and Testing

By providing a more comprehensive perspective on user interactions and experiences, this method goes beyond the conventional metrics-driven analysis. By highlighting the complementary nature of qualitative and quantitative data, mindful user research promotes a well-rounded understanding of the research process.

Active listening and open-ended questioning play a crucial role in this strategy of intentionally and thoughtfully acquiring user ideas. By paying close attention to the finer points of user feedback, this method is able to record not just the how and what of user interactions, but also their motivations. This method gives a more complete picture of the user's journey by giving weight to the feelings and narratives that drive their actions.

As part of their thoughtful user research, UX designers ask people probing questions to get to know them on a deeper level and see things from their point of view. This approach goes beyond simple questioning to foster an environment where users are not just acknowledged but also understood, and their input is not only documented but also treated with empathy.

> An attitude of true interest and a yearning to comprehend the user's reality describes mindful user research. It is about exploring the user's emotional and psychological characteristics, going deeper than just the surface-level replies. By putting themselves in the user's shoes, designers can have a better understanding of their wants and needs than what would be obvious from basic analytics or surface observations.

Even in usability testing, when watching how users interact with the product is only the first step, taking a conscious approach is essential. To conduct thoughtful usability testing, one must put themselves in the shoes of the product's users. It entails seeing how users react emotionally, their happiness, sadness, and perplexity as they use the interface.

Emotional journey testing seeks to understand the user's emotional journey through the product, rather than just finding pain points or usability concerns. Incorporating mindfulness into usability testing allows designers to better understand the product's impact on the user's life and emotions, and how to meet or exceed their expectations.

Creating Holistic and Inclusive Experiences

This method promotes a thorough examination of the wide range of users, pushing design beyond its traditional limits. To practice mindful inclusion in user experience, one must acknowledge and appreciate the wide range of user skills, backgrounds, and life circumstances. It is a way of thinking that aims to comprehend and meet the diverse range of human experiences and requirements.

By considering the consumer as a whole, we can make sure that digital products are relevant and usable for everyone, no matter their background or situation. It necessitates a strong dedication to learning about and accommodating the unique needs of various user demographics, including those with impairments.

Making sure that all users can easily access and use the experience is a crucial part of thoughtful UX design for developing inclusive experiences. For this reason, it is important to create user interfaces that are accessible to a wide range of abilities, including those of people with cognitive, motor, visual, or hearing impairments.

To make sure that all people can easily use and benefit from digital products, it is important to establish design principles that promote mindful inclusion. It is about making a product accessible to everyone, regardless of their language, physical impairments, or level of technological proficiency. This is how user experience designers make the internet a more inclusive and accepting place for everyone.

Integrating mindfulness into user experience design also entails creating with comprehension and empathy. This compassionate method entails attempting to understand the product from the users' points of view by placing oneself in their shoes.

To make sure the product connects with people on a deeper, more individual level, it is important to recognize and handle the emotional parts of the user experience. A product's emotional influence on users is considered alongside its utilitarian features in mindful UX's empathic design. The goal of this technique is to make people's lives easier by providing them with experiences that are useful, pleasant, and empowering in addition to being practical and easy.

When it comes to creating fair digital experiences, mindful inclusivity in UX design is also very important. In the digital era, designers help level the playing field by making products accessible and relevant to a wide range of users. To ensure that all users have an equal chance to reap the benefits of technological progress, this fair approach to design takes into account and resolves the cultural and social aspects of accessibility. The goal is to create digital goods that are inclusive and do not exacerbate existing disparities by thinking about the larger societal implications of the design process.

To sum up, user experience design that is holistic and inclusive aims to make digital products accessible to all people. Products developed by user experience designers that incorporate mindfulness and empathy into their work are more likely to meet people' varied needs while also being aesthetically pleasing and practical.

This chapter highlights how mindful inclusivity may revolutionize user experience design, leading to digital interactions that are more compassionate, fair, and focused on people. This piece beautifully captures the essence of a future when technology seamlessly blends with human variety, creating an inclusive digital landscape that benefits all users.

8.2 Present Awareness: Mindful Design Practices

The goal of practicing present awareness in user experience design is to encourage a high degree of involvement and focus all through the design process. This approach encourages a design practice that is fully present in the here and now by raising awareness of the impact of every choice.

By practicing mindfulness, designers are able to immerse themselves in their work and approach it from a new, objective angle. It is a method that not only makes designs more innovative and relevant, but also makes sure they are in perfect harmony with what people need right now and what technology can do.

Fully immersing oneself in the work at hand is essential for embracing current awareness in design. By deliberately avoiding interruptions and assumptions, designers who embrace this method provide their undivided attention to the creative process. When one is this absorbed in their job, they are able to give careful consideration to each detail of the design.

Being fully present allows designers to tackle every project with an open mind, unbound by preconceived notions or previous experiences. In the creative process, a new point of view is priceless since it lets designers investigate novel approaches and ideas that could otherwise go unnoticed.

One of the most important factors in user experience design decision-making is practicing present awareness. Designers can improve the quality of their decisions by practicing mindfulness and being completely present.

Thinking about how a design decision will affect the user experience is an important part of making thoughtful decisions. A more sophisticated comprehension of user behavior and preferences results from designers' increased sensitivity to the nuances of user interaction. Designing with this level of insight is essential for satisfying user wants and preventing problems in the future.

Another important factor in encouraging innovation and making sure designs are relevant is incorporating present awareness into UX design. Keep your mind on the here and now, and you will be more prepared to adapt to the ever-shifting tech scene and consumer expectations.

This method promotes keeping designs up-to-date in terms of usability and usefulness by constantly evaluating and adjusting them. By maintaining a state of constant self-awareness, designers are able to swiftly react to changing market conditions, consumer preferences, and technology developments by modifying their designs in real-time.

Cultivating a Mindful Design Environment

A crucial step in raising UX designers' level of present-moment awareness is the establishment of a mindful design environment. Developing the kind of sharp concentration and clear thinking that are foundational to mindful design is the goal of this purpose-built space.

Intentionally reducing the number of distractions in such a setting allows designers to give their undivided attention to the creative process. For designers to be able to focus intently on their work, this setting is essential for promoting profound concentration. The peaceful and well-organized mindful design area serves as a mental and physical work-station that promotes uninterrupted flow and innovation.

To cultivate a focused and clear attitude among designers, it is essential to incorporate mindfulness techniques into this mindful design environment. Incorporate mindfulness practices into your regular routine using techniques like guided meditation, mindful breathing, and meditation.

The ability to relax and concentrate is fundamental to any creative endeavor, and these activities might assist. Practicing mindfulness on a regular basis might help designers cleanse their minds of distractions and get a new perspective on their work. The attention and quality of the design work are a reflection of the benefits of mindfulness in the design environment, which include improved concentration and a sense of balance.

When people in a mindful design setting are able to concentrate and let go of distractions, new ideas and solutions can flourish. Free from the restraints of stress and mental fog, designers working in such a setting are better able to think creatively.

> Because of this conceptual clarity, designers are free to be more experimental and exploratory, increasing the likelihood that new, original ideas may emerge. Designers can immerse themselves more fully in their work, testing out ideas and methods with an open mind. Solutions that are both successful and innovative, focused on the needs of the user, are born from the union of mindfulness and design knowledge in this setting.

Because of its conduciveness to concentration, serenity, and mindfulness techniques, this setting is great for designers' ability to think clearly and creatively. Here, designers may unleash their creativity and solve real-world problems by devoting themselves fully to their work without interruption.

By incorporating this considerate mindset into the design process, user experience teams may make digital products that are highly responsive to consumers' wants, requirements, and emotions, in addition to being aesthetically beautiful and functional. In order to create user experiences that are considerate, sympathetic, and genuinely meaningful to the user community, this chapter stresses the significance of a mindful design environment.

Implementing Mindfulness in the Design Process

By incorporating mindfulness into UX design, we are moving away from the old, fast-paced ways and toward something far more methodical and reflective. By deliberately reducing the pace of the design process, this mindful methodology encourages more in-depth consideration of every facet of the final product.

The designers are able to give careful thought to each and every design detail when they work at a slower pace. The goal here is not inefficiency but rather making sure that everyone is aware of the consequences of their decisions.

> Designers are able to investigate several possibilities, consider multiple alternatives, and comprehend the possible consequences of their decisions when they move at a leisurely pace. Better solutions that are both innovative and in line with consumer expectations and needs are the result of a more deliberate and comprehensive design approach.

Being fully present in the here and now is essential to mindfulness as it pertains to user experience design. Being adaptable and responsive to changing conditions, feedback, and information is key to success in this area. Being adaptable and receptive to new ideas are hallmarks of mindful designers.

They have a firm grasp on the fact that their designs must evolve in response to ever-changing market situations, technology capabilities, and user demands. By keeping an open mind throughout the design process, you can include fresh insights gleaned from analytics, user input, or technical advancements. It requires a mindset that is always open to changing and improving ideas to make sure the end result is still useful and relevant for people today.

Cultivating an attitude of adaptability and constant development is also an important part of implementing mindfulness in UX design. Design, according to this view, is more of a process than a final product. Mindful designers are adaptable in their approach because they know there is always space for growth and development.

With this outlook, we can foster a culture of continuous improvement by regularly assessing and enhancing our designs. Recognizing that both user demands, and technology landscapes are always evolving, the method prioritizes progress and adaptation above perfection. To keep their products at the cutting edge of innovation and user happiness, UX teams should embrace this continual and adaptable approach to design.

Designers who practice mindfulness are able to make items that are thoughtful of the user's journey in addition to being aesthetically pleasing and practical. Focusing on the here and now allows us to create user experiences that are highly personalized to each individual's requirements and circumstances, as discussed in this chapter.

It promotes an approach to design that is reflective, adaptive, and ever-changing, so that digital products can be relevant when made but also have an influence and resonance in the digital world as it changes.

Mindful Collaboration and Communication

Present awareness has far-reaching implications for teamwork and communication in user experience design. Teams can work together more effectively and harmoniously when members practice mindfulness in these encounters.

An elevated degree of awareness and purpose in all kinds of communication characterizes mindful collaboration in user experience design. This method guarantees that conversations are chances for true understanding and connection rather than only information exchanges.

To foster a more in-depth examination of ideas and viewpoints, this setting encourages each team member to provide their undivided attention and participate actively. Through these considerate exchanges, we create a space where everyone feels comfortable voicing their opinions and where we can work together to develop answers to design problems that are fresh and truly represent our collective wisdom.

The importance of precise and well-understood communication is key to conscious collaboration. Being mindful while communicating within design teams is much more than simply getting your point across; it is also about making sure everyone understands and values your ideas for what they are.

To achieve this goal, one must make an effort to listen attentively, express themselves precisely, and look for common ground. When working in a mindful design environment, everyone in the team does their best to maintain an open mind during meetings. With this level of candor, ideas can flow more freely, and both parties can provide and receive constructive criticism that can only improve the team's work together. A culture of collaborative invention and creativity can flourish in such a setting since team members can build upon one another's ideas.

Being highly attuned to the team's dynamics is also an important component of mindful collaboration. This facet of mindfulness takes into account the fact that every team member is special in their own way and has specific requirements, as well as the fact that everyone on the team contributes something different.

An important part of the mindful design is recognizing and making use of people's unique perspectives and experiences. By viewing individual diversity as assets rather than liabilities, this method promotes an environment where team members are able to communicate with one another with empathy and respect.

In order to increase productivity, personal growth, and job happiness, teams should be attentive to the needs and abilities of each member. This will lead to a more inclusive and supportive work environment.

> User experience designers can cultivate an atmosphere that encourages comprehension, empathy, and clarity by encouraging present awareness in team interactions. In order to achieve cohesive and well-considered design outcomes, this chapter emphasizes the importance of attentive cooperation.

It demonstrates how a thoughtful strategy for collaboration may improve team dynamics, which in turn improves the design process and creates a more creative, harmonious, and productive workplace. In order to assemble a team that excels in both technical skill and emotional intelligence and teamwork, it is essential to practice mindful collaboration and communication.

The Impact of Present Awareness in UX Design

Designers may create digital experiences that break down barriers with this method, which is based on mindfulness principles. Through the incorporation of present awareness approaches, designers get the ability to craft solutions that are both innovative and in tune with users' current demands and realities.

In this chapter, we explore how mindfulness can greatly improve a designer's capacity for creativity, responsiveness, and effectiveness in the design process. Incorporating a thoughtful approach into design ensures that every detail is carefully studied, leading to solutions that are both technically solid and thoroughly in tune with consumers' expectations and experiences.

Designing user experiences with mindfulness has a significant impact on innovation. It promotes the idea that designers should tackle every project independently, unencumbered by previous patterns or assumptions.

Because of this receptivity, fresh and original ideas are able to grow. Additionally, designers are better able to adapt to the always- changing digital world when they are fully conscious of the here and now. Being completely in the here and now allows designers to swiftly adjust to shifting tastes, user feedback, and technology developments. Since the digital world is always changing, this nimbleness makes sure that the design solutions are both successful and interesting now and in the future.

Another way that UX designers can put the focus on the user is by including mindfulness practices. By staying in the now, designers are more likely to put themselves in the user's shoes, which results in more compassionate and easy-to-use designs. It is about getting to know the user's journey on a deeper level, beyond the utilitarian.

With this level of insight, we can design user-friendly digital experiences that also cater to and uplift users' emotional needs. Mindful design methods guarantee that digital goods are both efficient and enriching by concentrating on users' present demands and situations. This enhances the overall digital experience.

Incorporating this kind of consideration into the design process results in digital goods that are superior in terms of functionality and also strike a profound emotional and contextual chord with consumers. In order to cultivate a design approach that is inventive, user-centric, and reflective of the present moment, the chapter emphasizes the relevance of mindfulness.

By incorporating these practices into their work, user experience designers may make digital products that improve users' digital lives in every way, from the practical to the aesthetic. A digital world that is richer, more compassionate, and user-focused is the result of this strategy.

Harmonizing the Design Landscape

It is important to consider the distinctive and complementary combination of mindfulness principles and the
complexities of UX design as we near the end of this book.
Throughout this book, we have explored a world where the
ancient teachings of Buddhism meet the cutting-edge
practice of user experience design.

This investigation has revealed a way forward that is firmly based on human-centric principles and actively promotes innovation. Throughout the book, we have seen how mindfulness, empathy, and present awareness can revolutionize user experience design and take it to the next level. The end result is digital experiences that are strong in functionality and also touch people emotionally because of the depth and soundness of their ethics.

The quest to incorporate mindfulness into user experience design goes beyond personal practice and into the area of design community culture shift. A culture that values a thorough, compassionate knowledge of users and a constant dedication to inclusive and ethical design practices — these are the ideals that this book argues for as the foundation for a mindful design culture.

By encouraging a more meaningful relationship and active participation from users, this culture goes above and beyond the typical goals of design. By fully embracing this culture of mindful design, teams and designers can create products that meet users' wants and dreams, turning technology into a tool for improving people's lives.

The integration of mindfulness practices with user experience design has a significant effect on the design, development, and use of digital products. As a result of this integration, design thinking undergoes a sea change, evolving from an exclusively pragmatic to an approach that is compassionate, thoughtful, and conscious of ethical issues.

It recommends that designers be more self-aware as they work, thinking about how their designs would affect people in general as well as their specific target audience. By making mindfulness an integral part of user experience design, we can make digital products that help people emotionally and mentally as much as they help them physically.

Envisioning a Harmonious Digital Future

We are on the cusp of a new age in user experience design, and the lessons learned from *UX Design Through the Buddha's Eyes* point the way to a more compassionate and cooperative online environment.

> The emphasis here goes beyond efficiency and aesthetics to include the more fundamental principles of mindfulness, compassion, and ethical integrity, which is a radical departure from traditional paradigms of design. According to this book, in the future, user experience designers will be more than just builders of digital interfaces; they will also be advocates for a more inclusive digital environment and protectors of user health. From this vantage point, the future of the internet is one in which technology is responsible and caring, improving people's lives for the better.

There is a need for a paradigm change in thinking and doing as we go on the path to include mindfulness principles into user experience design. With this change comes a reevaluation of design's fundamental goals, with user satisfaction taking precedence over product form and function.

Despite this, the UX industry is about to face enormous chances for growth and innovation thanks to these problems. Mindfulness training allows creatives to tap into previously untapped reservoirs of inspiration, allowing them to build cutting-edge digital experiences that also strike a chord with users on an emotional and meaningful level.

Mindfulness integration into user experience design is a challenging but potentially life-changing endeavor. The text emphasizes the need for designers to think beyond the box and prioritize user-centricity and ethical considerations alongside technological expertise. By taking this revolutionary step, we can reimagine what it means to be a designer and create digital experiences that better reflect the human experience.

We have the chance to improve our professional practice and help shape a digital world that is more thoughtful, understanding, and user-focused if we rise to the difficulties that come with working in this dynamic industry.

Inviting readers on a profound journey towards rethinking UX design, this is more than just a guide. We are embarking on a quest to create a digital landscape that is balanced and enriched by combining the technical aspects of user experience with the profound teachings of Buddhism. It promotes a dynamic method of design that combines attentive practice with ongoing education.

By recognizing the interdependence of our digital and physical environments, this method seeks to design digital experiences that go beyond mere efficiency to enhance, engage, and elevate the human experience.

Finally, this book has shown us the way forward for a digital world that is more user-centric, sympathetic, and harmonious. These pages lay out a thoughtful and caring approach to user experience design that will make this future a reality, not just a faraway fantasy.

The next step is crystal clear: integrate mindful practices into our design workflows, never stop learning, and dedicate ourselves fully to making digital experiences that enrich the human experience in a globally interconnected world.

About the Author

ERIC INFANTI

Currently serving as the UX/UI Design Manager for Combined Arms, a nonprofit dedicated to veterans' well-being, Eric brings over 30 years of expertise in information technology design. With a tech-savvy foundation, he possesses the knowledge to build web-based environments & portals and launch online products and a crucial skill set of wisdom in mindfulness meditation.

Eric's transformative programs are meticulously crafted for individuals and businesses, creating a harmonious fusion of mind, body, and spirit. Harnessing the potent synergy of this amalgamation, he propels human performance to unprecedented heights, fostering enduring well-being and resilience.

A U.S. Marine Corps Veteran and accomplished eleven-time author, Eric, known for his works such as *Marine in the Mat, Yoga for the Jiu-Jitsu Athlete*, and *Breath Becomes Life*, he brings a wealth of knowledge to guide others on their healing journey. Passionate about alleviating the struggles of those with PTSD and related communities, he offers comprehensive integral coaching programs, seamlessly integrating mindfulness, resiliency, yoga, meditation, and movement.

With a rich background encompassing over 2,000 hours of yoga teacher & meditation training and dual master's degrees in *Buddhist Psychology* and *Ayurvedic Medicine*, and is a Ph.D. candidate with a study on the *Role of Extreme Athletic Peak Flow States on Resilience and Professional Outcomes*.

Eric is a seasoned teacher of Iyengar, Ashtanga, Vinyasa, and Yin Yoga. His training in Mysore, India, under the guidance of Sri K. Pattabhi Jois's family and Acharya V. Sheshadri, reflects a commitment to deepening his understanding of the body-mind-spirit connection.

Eric's journey began with a clear vision and a desire to create a life aligned with his dreams. Despite many challenges and uncertainties, he persevered, taking intentional steps toward self-reflection, self-education, and self-discovery. Empowered by this wisdom, he has successfully navigated the complexities of the human condition to support others.

As a result, Eric stands today as a beacon of empowerment, changing lives through his passion. Through his work, he extends an invitation to beautiful souls like you, inspiring them to embark on their unique journey of transformation and fulfillment.

www.ingramcontent.com/pod-product-compliance
Lightning Source LLC
LaVergne TN
LVHW041212050326
832903LV00021B/591